LETHAL LOVE

Indiana Studies in Biblical Literature
Herbert Marks and Robert Polzin,
general editors

LETHAL LOVE

Feminist Literary Readings of Biblical Love Stories

MIEKE
BAL

INDIANA UNIVERSITY PRESS
BLOOMINGTON & INDIANAPOLIS

For Suzanne Koster

Manufactured in the United States of America

Library of Congress Cataloging-in-Publication Data

Bal, Mieke, 1946–
Lethal love.

(Indiana studies in biblical literature)
Translation of: Femmes imaginaires.
Bibliography: p.
Includes index.
1. Women in the Bible. 2. Bible—Hermeneutics.
3. Criticism. 4. Bible and feminism. I. Title.
II. Series.
BS575.B2913   1987   220.6'088042   86-45592
ISBN 0-253-33323-7
ISBN 0-253-20434-8 (pbk.)

3 4 5 6 7 97 96 95 94 93

CONTENTS

PREFACE

This book is a thoroughly revised version of *Femmes Imaginaires*, which appeared simultaneously in Utrecht (HES), Montréal (HMH), and Paris (Nizet) in 1986. The French version aimed primarily at revising narrative theory in the light of ideology-critique, specifically feminism. The English version reverses the accents; it is first and foremost a study of biblical love stories and the ways we read them. As a result, the theoretical sections have been abridged and the interpretations made more autonomous.

Previous versions of some of the chapters have been published before. Chapter 1 appeared as "The Semiotics of Symmetry, or the Use of Hermeneutic Models" in *v/s Versus* 35–36 (1983); chapter 2 as "The Rhetoric of Subjectivity" in *Poetics Today* 5, 2 (1984); chapter 5 under the same title in *Poetics Today* 6, 1–2 (1985), also published by Harvard University Press as *The Female Body in Western Culture*, ed. Susan R. Suleiman.

Most of the work on this book was done within the framework of the new Program of Women's Studies in Letters, at the Rijksuniversiteit Utrecht. Invitations to the Université de Montréal and the Université du Québec à Montréal stimulated much of my thinking on these matters. The final version was completed at Harvard University, in the Program of Women's Studies in Religion and the Department of Hebrew Bible, and under the auspices of the Ford Foundation.

Of the many persons who have, at one stage or another of the work, been of indispensable help, I can mention only a few. In the first place, Fokkelien van Dijk and Grietje van Ginneken; without them, I would not have turned toward the biblical stories at all. Ann Jefferson and Terence Cave, Deirdre and Tom Burton, helped me at the other end of the line, and offered valuable criticism on what I then thought to be the final version. Not so; the precious advice so generously given by Gilbert Chaitin had a fortunate influence on the text as it is now. Throughout the enterprise, Ria Lemaire and Ernst van Alphen have been indispensably stimulating and critical. I thank them all.

I dedicate this book to my mother, the keenest of my readers.

LETHAL LOVE

INTRODUCTION

Literary theory, feminism, and narrative theory are the three discourses that meet in this study. They intersect at the point where all three are preoccupied with thinking through the relations that constitute the problematics of human life and language. Rather than the dominance or subservience of any one of them, the possibility of mutual illumination is presupposed.

The object of this study is confrontation. It is about the interaction of the various responses constituting the reception of biblical love stories. I will stress the ambiguities that the texts allow and contrast them with disambiguated rewritings of various kinds. A few possible interpretations of my enterprise should be eliminated from the start.

First, I do not claim the Bible to be either a feminist resource or a sexist manifesto. That kind of assumption can be an issue only for those who attribute moral, religious, or political authority to these texts, which is precisely the opposite of what I am interested in. It is the cultural function of one of the most influential mythical and literary documents of our culture that I discuss, as a strong representative instance of what language and literature can do to a culture, specifically to its articulation of gender. Second, the confrontation is not meant to "restore" an "original" or even a privileged meaning. Such an attempt is self-contradictory—and here, too, the Bible is an exemplary case—since the illusion of origin is disturbed by the evidence of textual criticism. Edmund Leach (1983) uses the irreverent phrase "unscrambling the omelette" to describe the attempt. Third, I do not mean to demonstrate how modern narrative theory replaces the divine voice as the authority that fixes meaning. Nor would I agree with those biblical scholars who claim that the poetics of the Bible is so alien to our theories that the latter are pointless in relation to the former. Such cultural relativism veils an as yet unresolved belief in the authority of origin. A dialogue between the two, at the risk of disturbing the presuppositions of both, is, as I hope to demonstrate, a more promising procedure.

The motives for eliminating these three possible interpretations of the enterprise are interrelated. I wish to make a case for *difference*. As a first

1

consequence, the relative arbitrariness of all readings, including the sexist readings we have become so used to, will come to the fore. It is my contention that, in spite of major differences in the innumerable readings of the Bible, there has been in Christian, Western culture a continuous line toward what I refer to as "the dominant reading": a monolithically misogynist view of those biblical stories wherein female characters play a role, and a denial of the importance of women in the Bible as a whole. Let me add right away that this does not imply that all female characters are seen as negative; quite the contrary. It does imply that any positive view of a female character has to be reevaluated for its recuperation within male interests. Evidence for the existence of such a dominant reading can be sought first and foremost in popularized "uses" of biblical material. Two obvious examples may suffice at this point, both further elaborated in this book: Ruth and Eve. Both characters have a mixed reputation, Eve's predominantly negative, Ruth's more positive. If the latter is generally praised for her loyalty to her Hebrew mother-in-law, she does receive some criticism for her daring seduction of Boaz. My reading of the Book of Ruth will challenge these two opinions. Ruth deserves praise, not only for her loyalty but also for her "kindness" toward Boaz, the man who is seen as her benefactor but whose benefactor I claim she is in her turn. Eve, sometimes seen as the Ur-mother, is mainly considered the *femme fatale*, temptress of man and the cause of human misery, her derivative birth being a prime symptom of her, and hence woman's, inferior status. I will defend a different reading, one that implies neither Eve's secondary birth nor her temptation. The equality of the simultaneous creation of man and woman out of a non-gendered first being, Eve's wisdom in her acceptance of the human condition, and her guiding of man will be among the discoveries of my alternative interpretation. Neither Ruth's goodness nor Eve's wickedness can be taken for granted; both views serve specific gender interests.

Is there, then, a dominant reading of the Bible? It can be argued that, in spite of the popularized views I take as my starting point, there are, and there have been throughout the history of exegesis, a myriad of different interpretations, scholarly, theological, and philosophical. I contend that the majority of these different readings nevertheless have some form or other of misogyny in common, even if they try hard, sometimes explicitly, to avoid it. Yes, I will give examples throughout this book. To start with the most paradoxical: Phyllis Trible's interpretation of Ruth (1978), in spite of its feminist intentions, does not escape the dominance of male interests. Nor do well-intended literary or scholarly readings. If, for the sake of my argument, I sometimes appear to be overgeneralizing, I will carefully enhance the specific content and impact of each of my sample readings. But the existence of a dominant reading, and the exceptions to it, are not my main concern. My focus will be on the *guidelines* that have been followed by a reader, and the intimate relationship between those guidelines and some form of male interest, rather than on sexism as such. I do not doubt that between popular views and scholarly interpretations the relation of information is mutual, to say the least; often, it is the popular view that the scholarly work will want to support, rather than the other way around. My choice of both popular and scholarly, reflective and less reflective forms of reception, from which I will set off the difference, is motivated by this interesting question of influence and the cultural anchoring of scholarship.

The alternative readings I will propose should not be considered as yet another, superior interpretation that overthrows all the others. My goal is rather to show, by the sheer possibility of a different reading, that "dominance" is, although present and in many ways obnoxious, not unproblematically established. It is the challenge rather than the winning that interests me. For it is not the sexist interpretation of the Bible as such that bothers me. It is the possibility of dominance itself, the attractiveness of coherence and authority in culture, that I see as the source, rather than the consequence, of sexism. For one thing, it allows for deviance to a certain extent, because deviance can be so easily accommodated, recuperated. One example of this mechanism, which at the same time counters the accusation of a biased and limited choice of samples, is Hugo's poem "Booz endormi," based on the Book of Ruth. The poem is deviant from the view of Boaz as benefactor; it stresses Boaz's own needs. The interpretations of the poem are, however, related to the dominant interpretation of Ruth, rather than being based on a detailed reading of the relationship between the poem and the biblical work.

The analysis of Ruth starts off as a double inversion. The later metatext of Hugo is taken as a starting point, a move that reverses the chronological order but provides a clue to the moves of reading itself; and the privileging of the global, the normal, the "important," is given over to the minute, the trivial, the apparently trivial, in what Naomi Schor calls a "clitoral hermeneutics." Schor's work (1984) is in my view one of the clearest and most convincing cases to date for such a feminist deconstruction of literary priorities, and the reader will find many reminiscences of her thought in the present study.

These considerations lead to the question that underlies this study. Is there a relation between ideological dominance and specific forms of representation? I will argue that there is, and in each of the five chapters of this book I will examine a different, small-scale aspect of representation in its narrative modes in order to substantiate the overall claim. Thus the enhancing of difference as a means of deconstructing the dominance of male-centeredness in the reading of these highly influential texts will take specific forms, each time focusing on a crucial aspect of narrative structure as the "entrance" into difference.

Dominance and difference are polemically engaged in those cultural processes which the analysis of narrative necessarily deals with. In the early sixties, Roland Barthes convincingly argued for the intimate relationship between realist representation and the imposition of ideological values. His early studies on myth (1957) must be confronted with some of his views on realism (1964) in order to evaluate the power of the mechanism he denounced. In his article "L'effet du réel" he displays the very dominance of the priorities he denounces elsewhere. When dealing with the detail in realist representation, such as the nonintegrated, superfluous "connotator of reality," he follows, rather than deconstructing, the moves of the realist author. Instead, a systematic assignment of priority to "meaningless" details will invert the values of representation, thus bringing them to the fore. In the present study, the realist fallacy our culture has adopted will be shown at work. The belief in the unproblematic representation of an "objective reality" is far from being extinct. It is constantly there, underlying scholarly arguments and manipulative rewritings. It is my claim that biblical narrative is not, or need not be read as, realist fiction. It has a self-reflexive quality that allows for a reading that displays, through its own inconsistencies, the gaps and failures of realism.

If, in Barthes's view, myth and ideology are synonymous, it is because of the power of realist representation in the perpetuation of values. Myth is, in this conception, another form of realism, not "geographical," showing that the reality around us is "like this," but historical, claiming that what is now has always been. It posits the return to origins, from the point of view of a "retrospective fallacy" that I will discuss in the last chapter. Current views of myth confirm and perpetuate this notion. Edmund Leach, for example, defines myths, in line with Malinowski (1948), as "charters for social action" (1983), as "sacred tales about past events which are used to justify social action in the present." This functionalist view does consider myth as an ideological agent. As such, it sounds critical enough. It has, however, problems that confirm the strong dominance of the ideological concerns it tries to analyze. The "past events" are uncritically assumed, for example. Asking oneself whether or not the events have taken place, a problem undecidable and irrelevant, is doing exactly what myth wants us to do: to accept, while wondering about what "really happened," the projection of present values into a narrative form that provides them with existential evidence. The modifier "sacred" is not only a quite correct description of the framework within which myth is used but also, if not further analyzed, a justification through the respectability it assigns to it. Moreover, it enhances a permanency that, as I have argued elsewhere, is not at all characteristic of myths (1987). Far from remaining the same in the course of history, mythical texts are constantly changed, and can be so precisely because they have, in the view of culture, the aura of permanency that the definition confirms. This fallacy of permanency, which mediates between the "geographical" and the "historical" realisms, is also visible on another level. Not only does it justify myth's effort to prevent social action from being taken, in favor of the status quo, but it enables myth to defend the interests of the dominating groups.

One point in particular has to be stressed: the events of the past that are represented in the sacred tales in order to orient social action are not necessarily major political events, nor are they always successful. If the establishment of the people of Israel out of a tribal society is one obvious reading of the Bible, there is, nevertheless, room for problematic events, or even for problems. The dominating patriarchal system is represented as originating "in the past," on the one hand, but as being highly problematic in its consequences on the other. It is this insecurity that seems to me the most underestimated mythical meaning of the Bible, and it is the traces of this insecurity within the fractured texts that I am trying to map out.

Reading is an encounter between several subjects, and that encounter is going to be, in this book, the *site* of the tensions I want to study. Subjects are all over the place in contemporary theory, and it seems useful to analyze how and where they function in the processing of narrative. The reader of biblical love stories is particularly handicapped by the confused and confusing position of relating to stories that he or she already knows, through the action of other subjects. The stories are *about* subjects, characters who stand in a tense, ambivalent relation to one another that we call love, without knowing too well what we mean by that. They also are embedded in a complex structure that mediates their adventures. It will be shown that it is emphatically the subjective structure of the texts that is subjected to a reorganizing and deeply destabilizing activity of the reading and rewriting subject. In a field that has been predominantly a male prerogative, these stories, which deal with the very tensions that privilege is motivated by, cannot but have undergone ideological adaptation. The female subject has been repressed or made guilty of all that did not fit; as a result, the stories, problematic in their ancient versions, have become less problematic, smoother, but also less interesting, in their modern cultural uses. The following analyses will focus on the structural positions of subjects in the stories, in the events they tell, in the processing of the texts. In order to make a plausible case, a concept of the *semiotic* subject will be presented as a possible mediator between textual, narrative subjects and the "real" subjects that deal with them, use them, and are influenced by them.

Why love stories? Not only because they tell the myths about gender relations, although this obvious motivation cannot be forgotten. There is more to it. As the discussion of the concept of myth showed, the ways of the mythical fallacies—origin, permanency, "historical" and "geographical" realism—are based on a tension that seems to underlie all the fields my study tries to interrelate. The two realisms, notably, serve to resolve a tension between analogy and chronology, between sameness and difference, that, as the analyses will demonstrate, is crucial for the mythical process to take place at all. It is also crucial for love itself, as others have amply argued. And it is crucial for narrative, where the line of continuity, the linearity that is supposed to distinguish verbal from visual representation, can function only within a recurring assessment of analogons. It is within this tension that structure receives meaning and that meaning is proposed through structure. The tension between the stories and their rewritings, then, becomes emblematic of the tensions they deal with: assumed to be the same, they are only analogous to their previous versions, and it is the diachronic difference, rather than the permanent or original truth, that can be socially active in the Leachian sense.

The priority of difference that will be my guideline does not allow me to propose any unified claim about either the Bible or the readings of it. The stories I analyze are often not connected to one another; they are not presented in a chronological order, and they do not represent the same view of "love." The readers' responses selected come from different periods, from different countries, levels of discourse, and disciplinary backgrounds. This variety is not meant to convey an implicit claim of unity. In each case, the goal is to analyze principles of reading, types of arguments, types of silences. One reading has been selected for its status as a respectable academic performance (chap. 1); another, for its widespread acceptance in popular culture (chap. 2); others for their exceptional inversion of the more common proceedings (chap. 3), or their influence on biblical scholarship and the resulting views of the Bible (chap. 4). The last chapter is the only one where the reading is considered as a founding text, as an influential phase in the transition from Judaism to Christianity: Paul's statement on women. Even there, my concern is with what "Paul" did, which shifts and reversals he made in his reading of what was his founding text. It is not my claim that all these readers are similarly sexist or patriarchal; rather, as I indicated before, I claim that the reading fallacies they adopt, regardless of their differences, all lead to a position that participates in the repression of women, which they share with the different forms of patriarchy. I understand patriarchy as the social and ideological repression of women in favor of the domination of men, as well as the domination of older over younger men, and I argue that specific forms of representation inform these repressions.

The preceding principles have led me to present a work whose heterogeneity is part of its project. There is a line to my overall argument, but it is a cursory and tortuous one. Starting from the basic question of why we need methods at all, I will argue in the first chapter for narrative theory as a hermeneutic tool that leads the interpreter to convincing results. Criteria will be discussed, methods compared, and the problematic case of David's moral fall analyzed. The woman, in that story, is turned from victim into killer, at will. In the second chapter the method will be further elaborated in view of its *critical* capacities. It will be criticized in its turn by the same move. The concept of the subject as the place where the tensions between chronology and analogy meet is also the focal point of the critical dimension I seek to argue for. Gender ideologies will be interpreted, this time within the psychoanalytic framework, which relativizes and transforms the concept of heroism. Samson becomes the exemplary ambiguous hero, a position that entails the same ambiguity for Delilah's presumed wickedness, and a paradoxical reversal of both characters' positions becomes possible.

The third chapter starts from poetic reception, discusses the limits of text-internal analysis by the use of metatextuality as a hermeneutic device, and thus demonstrates the impossibility of either position in the synchrony-diachrony debate. The Book of Ruth provides an example in that a text-internal interpretation cannot but take the status of the book itself into account, which is metatextual, and hence opens the text up beyond itself.

The concept of chronology as it has been interpreted in narrative theory will be discussed in the fourth chapter. It shows the contradictions inherent in time (Ricoeur 1983). Textual criticism and its relevance are at stake in the study of the sequence of Gen. 37–39, where the chronological line seems disturbed. The thematic approach proposed by Alter (1981) provides only a partial solution, since, based as it is on analogy, it ignores chronology when the latter is ambiguous. We will see that Tamar, although she did not know young Joseph, is indispensable for the understanding of the youth's adventures.

Because character is both the most central and the most problematic concept of narrative theory, its relations to the tensions alluded to will be used in the last chapter to illuminate the contradictions of narrative theory itself. The first of all female characters, the woman in Gen. 1–3, and her adventures as a cultural representative of the problematics of sexism, emblematize in the end the new beginning that critical studies of gender and culture can help to bring about.

The line of my argument, which moves from a positive choice of a methodology, through its ongoing problematization, toward a rather negative conclusion, is, I hastily add, meant to suggest not the pointlessness of narrative theory but rather the power of its self-critical capacities.

This study suffers from the same tensions that I have been discussing throughout this preface. Each chapter is similar to, and different from, the others, and the order of the sequence is both important and random. As for sameness, each segment consists of a confrontation between several discourses: the biblical love story, a sample of its reception, a critical concept under scrutiny, a hermeneutic framework, and an aspect of the method proposed and criticized at the same time. Table 1 plots the distribution of these elements. If the reader can be convinced that the gender ideologies that sustain culture today are no more self-evident than the authority of the Bible or the certainties of narrative theory and criticism, my study will have accomplished its main goal.

(Quotations are from the Authorized Version, unless otherwise indicated.)

Table 1

Chapter	Love Story	Type of Reception	Hermeneutic Framework	Concepts Used and Criticized	Aspects of Method Discussed
1	David & Bathsheba (the victim)	literary scholarship	narratology	symmetry, frame/gap	methodological status, heuristic value
2	Samson & Delilah (the helper)	children's Bibles, popular exegesis	psychoanalysis	hero/opponent	subject/ subjectivity
3	Ruth & Boaz (cooperation)	artistic reception (poetry, painting)	history	proper name, "mise en abyme"	metatextuality
4	Judah & Tamar (struggle)	textual criticism, thematics	plot-oriented interpretation	order, sequence	analogy/ chronology
5	Adam & Eve (development)	Christian mythology	formalism	character	critique of ideology

· 1 ·

THE EMERGENCE OF THE
LETHAL WOMAN, OR THE USE
OF HERMENEUTIC MODELS

Pregnancy and the Limits of Power

2 Sam. 11 narrates a story of sex and war, concealment and murder, the use of a woman and the abuse of power. Staying behind in Jerusalem while his army is fighting far away under the command of Joab, King David one evening perceives a beautiful woman and wants her. Since he is powerful, he has her. She becomes pregnant. David tries to cover up the fruit of the adultery by using the woman's husband. The man refuses, out of solidarity with his comrades at the front. Then David has him killed, under the pretext of war. He marries the woman. She is Bathsheba, the wife of Uriah the Hittite.

So far, this summary is not in conflict with the common view of this grim love story. It is consistent, for example, with two scholarly readings that I will discuss in this chapter. Although one scholar comes to the text as a biblical specialist while the two authors of the other piece are literary scholars, both analyses are works of literary criticism. They pay much attention to the structure of the text and are sensitive to its symmetries, its suspense, its irony, its imagery. It is the latter aspect that will chiefly retain us here—imagery as a problem, that is.

The text has one line that both sample critics consider problematic. Since they dwell on it extensively, the line, problematic because of a metaphor, makes a good case for the priority of the detail and its treatment in readers' response. The problematic verse is line 21. In his instruction to the messenger who is to report to David about the murder of Uriah, Joab suddenly inserts the following metaphor: "Who smote Abimelech the son of Jerubbesheth? did not a woman cast a piece of a millstone upon him from the wall, that he died in Thebez?" Both analyses we will discuss stress the apparent irrelevance of the metaphor, and the complex narrative structure in which it is embedded. Who is compared to whom here?

David, the mighty king, to Abimelech the usurper? Uriah, the humble soldier, to Abimelech the king? The raped woman to the woman who kills, to the lethal woman of Judg. 9:53? The confusion of the subjects compared is paralleled by the narrative structure itself: Who is speaking? Joab, to the messenger, to David? David, through Joab? Both problems are interrelated: the position of the woman in the metaphor depends on the involvement of the speaker and the addressee with the "problem" of the woman in the story.

On the one hand we have here a text, a love story. Within the relations of power that are at stake in this story, we cannot even distinguish between "love" and "rape," so that our referring to the text as a love story is ironic. On the other hand, we have two readings, both modern, scholarly, competent, interesting. Good literary criticism. The problem the text poses to these and other readers is a literary problem. It has to do with the figurative speech, with narrative, with the use of language: speech acts. It also, as if by accident, has to do with gender, violence, and power. It will be our task in this chapter to follow the long and tortuous path that leads from literary scholarship to gender ideology. The starting points are twofold. On the one hand, the detail of this textual problem will motivate our search. On the other hand, the broad and basic question of method will inform it, in a mutual challenge.

The question that will remain constant throughout this chapter will be, What happens, in this story, between male and female subjects, on all levels of representation? The question will limit our concerns to an extremely partial and political interest, the one that motivates my analysis. This practical approach is reflected in the section titles, which are meant to show the centrality of *use* as the mediation between language, representation, and social reality. The first uses examined are those of methods, of what I call hermeneutic models: the theoretical assumptions, more or less explicit, that direct our interpretations. The question asked and answered is, What is the use of such models? But also, What use, or abuse, can be and is made of them?

The Use of Interpretation

Interpreters of literary texts often claim to account for the reading process. They set up theories of the literary text as a foundation of their interpretations and present them implicitly or explicitly as models of how readers proceed when reading a text. These theories have, however, a self-fulfilling side to them. They describe how texts can be read if readers follow the conventions that underlie those hermeneutic models. They do not account for the freedom to follow variable conventions.

They are, as such, interesting enough. Jonathan Culler (1981) pleads for an approach to reading that would study exactly those conventions which ground the models, in order to account for the process of reading and interpretation. Interpretation models are in this view an object of study, on the same level as the resulting interpretations. While the defenders of the models-as-an-explanation-of-reading would consider models to be on a level different from that of interpretations, Culler would rather consider models as an implicit *direction for use* followed by those interpreters who believe in the model. Thus conceived, the semiotics of reading is a metasemiotics.

Culler's refusal to evaluate comparatively the different critical approaches is consistent with his goal: "to spell out the assumptions and interpretative operations that lead from text to interpretation." Hasty evaluation would be based on other assumptions and would therefore blur the distinction between criticism and metacriticism that is the foundation of this semiotics of reading. Culler convincingly argues that, for example, Jauss (1975), Mailloux (1978), and Fish (1971) cannot avoid this problem. As a result, they present their own interpretations as competitive with those they study, and they do so without completely and explicitly comparing their own and others' assumptions.

The semiotics of reading as outlined in Culler's article is an urgent task of literary scholarship. If exclusively practiced, however, it might soon have a paralyzing effect on the progress of criticism itself. First, in spite of Culler's mild and respectful opinions, critics may come to feel their work to be less worthy, since it is, more than they previously believed, ruled by conventions and based on assumptions they did not consciously choose. Second, the very refusal, highly justified and desirable as it is, of evaluating interpretations may discourage the critic because it rules out competition, thus hampering progress. Third, the critical work may seem irrelevant, even if only used as material for metacriticism, for, quantitatively speaking, there is already more than enough material available for such a semiotics of reading.

Of course, these reactions would be unjustified, since Culler's method was never meant to be imperialistic. Approaches to the literary text, whether or not they will subsequently be considered as evidence of particular reading strategies, can derive their standards from different goals. One modest and legitimate goal has always been a fuller understanding of the text, one that is sophisticated, reproducible, and accessible to a larger audience. As long as by "a fuller understanding" one means having found a more satisfying way of integrating the reading experience into one's life, more possibilities of doing something with this experience, such an approach is a justifiable critical practice.

In this view, the criteria for the evaluation of interpretations are the

traditional standards of plausibility, adequacy, and relevance. These criteria are basically pragmatic. Far from having anything to do with standards of "scientificity," they deal with what readers can find of use. An
interpretation will be judged *plausible* if it is based as explicitly as possible
on assumptions readers can share—if the interpretation is, within the
framework of those assumptions, felt to be dealing with the readers'
experience of the text. *Adequacy* will be acknowledged if the interpretation, at every stage of its unfolding, is connected with those textual
features the reader judges important, and which he or she considers as
"facts," however elusive the factual may be in the perception of discourse. Furthermore, the connections will have to be convincingly argued. *Relevance* is judged by the reader on the basis of his or her view of
the world. The relevance of a materialistic reading may totally escape the
notice of a reader who rejects the idea that economic issues and the
relations of power they produce could to a large extent determine the
structure of society. Psychoanalytical interpretations are often rejected
because the readers do not admit that, as Freud put it, "man is no master
in his own house." If a person does not believe in the unconscious, he or
she will find an account of unconscious meanings irrelevant.

An interpretation that is judged by a considerable number of readers
to meet these, and doubtless other, criteria will be found acceptable. This
acceptance can be a minimal justification of the critical work. Further
competition may arise in relation to the *progress of knowledge.* Usually, the
interpretation that explains the most "textual problems"—that is, features that readers feel uncomfortable with, that they cannot integrate
into their overall reading, like our disturbing metaphor—is found to be
the best one. Traditionally, that criterion has been based on the convention of *unity* (Van Alphen 1987), but this need not be so. It is sometimes
possible to give a convincing interpretation of such a problem only if it is
detached from the rest of the text. In fact, deconstructionist critics stress
inconsistencies in the text, thus creating a new, plausible way of dealing
with textual problems (for an introduction, see Belsey 1980; Culler
1983).

Another comparative criterion is the *surplus requirement.* Interpretations that are plausible, adequate, and relevant in general may fail to
meet with a positive reception because they have nothing new to say.
This is a commonsense standard, as well as a serious scientific one. Comparing different interpretations of one text, readers are entitled to ask
which one "taught them the most," that is, which one gave them the most
to think about, made them experience the text as most enriching, and so
on.

Of course, these standards are based on conventional assumptions
about literature, like the one, for example, that literature is psychologi-

cally and socially useful in that it is an exercise in open-mindedness, or, for others, a weapon in the service of conservative values. The desire for an explaining-away interpretation, instead of a deconstructive one, would probably be influenced by one's preference for conservatism as opposed to an awareness of possibilities of change. In both cases, we will find that a better understanding of literature as a social fact will be gained by an explicit account of the connection between the interpretive gesture and the political and psychological makeup of the person who performs it.

Hermeneutic models do not explain the reading process. They function on other levels. They shape understandings; they allow readers to grasp their own intuitive interpretations and make them accessible to others. They are tools for articulation. On a metacritical level, they produce the discourse that allows us to grasp the assumptions that structure critical understanding, e.g., Culler's project. Evaluation of models takes place on a metacritical level, according to various standards. From a socially oriented point of view, models may, for example, be judged according to the degree to which they allow readers to accommodate the different interpretations within their own cognitive possibilities, in order to help them to live with the text. Conversely, the models may be judged by how effectively they encourage readers to look at reality with unusual conceptions, that is, how well they train open-mindedness. From a critical point of view, standards are related to the goals of criticism itself. Models will be required to provide the critic with heuristic tools that work. Those tools are meant to span the gap between the general theoretical framework that the critic chooses to work with and the specific interpretations that the framework allows one to articulate. Those heuristic devices determine to a large extent the possible results, even if the competence, the psychological makeup, and the ideological stance of the critic have a decisive influence that is difficult to grasp.

Since the suspicion has arisen that the problematic detail of 2 Sam. 11:21 is somehow related to both gender ideology and representation, it seems likely that the interpretation of textual problems is a relevant issue in the use of models. Questions that arise, then, are the following:

—Does the model provide analytic and descriptive tools that allow the interpretation to be plausible, adequate, and relevant, to explain textual problems, and to give surplus information?
—Does the model prevent, or help prevent, interpretations from being implausible, inadequate, and irrelevant, from giving only information that we already have, and from repressing textual problems?

The importance of the second question has to be stressed. Quite often, models seem better than they are because they meet the first criterion, while their falling short in regard to the second one is overlooked.

Paradoxically, however, it is the second question that allows us to distinguish not only between useful and useless models but also between modeled and unmodeled interpretations, that is, between reproducible, teachable procedures and ad hoc performances. This point is important as it differentiates between empowering and intimidating interpretations. An unmodeled but seductive interpretation will be rhetorically powerful; students have no choice but to accept what seems appealing but is beyond their control. Modeled interpretations teach students not only what is interesting about the particular text but also how to deal with those things in other texts. Ultimately, the process of reading the Bible in freshman classes can be used to teach students more (or less) than "about" the Bible. If teachers show students what they do and why—in other words, if their interpretations are modeled—the student will be able to evaluate what is offered as a possible reading. When confronted with an unargued interpretation offered as the best, the only possible one, just because it comes so self-evidently, the student perpetuates the ideology offered without being aware of it.

In the following sections, I will briefly present three models of interpretation. These presentations are meant to provide the evaluation of the readings of the textual problem in the story of David and Bathsheba with just enough background to measure the impact of the models on the results.

The first model is the one that assumes a decisive influence of form over meaning, often referred to as formalism, but more adequately referred to as the *semiotics of form*, since it is ultimately the meaning and effect of the form that informs the subsequent interpretations. The different elaborations of the basic idea of the semiotics of form are numerous. One of the most representative, refined, and well-founded ones is Lotman's. The rival model is the equally generalized frame-theory. While the semiotics of form takes the signs in the text extremely seriously, the frame-theory-based models start at the other end, with the prior knowledge of the reader. It will be demonstrated that both models meet to a considerable extent the criteria outlined above, while they also illustrate, each on different grounds, some of the very dangers they accuse each other of incurring. My conclusions, negative as they are toward the cognitive claims, will be moderately positive regarding the possible fruitfulness of both models. At the same time, I will demonstrate that both of them partially fail with respect to a textual problem because they imply too strongly the convention of unity, problematic in itself.

The Use of Form

The semiotic foundation of the concept of form reached full maturity in the work of Lotman. In spite of the problem of the spatial metaphor inherent in the concept of form, most semioticians agree that, rather than expressing a content, a sign models its content. This conception implies that semantic elements are no longer clearly differentiated (Lotman 1977:21), since what is syntagmatic on one level may be semantic on another. Lotman claims this to be a feature of artistic texts. I thoroughly disagree with any such claim of semiotic literariness. In general, however, it is justifiable to assume that everything in a discourse can be meaningful, and that conventions allow readers to assume a special density of meaning in artistic texts. Readers can, on the basis of (1) the text and (2) their conventional expectations, attribute to each text a particular system of denotata, which is "not a copy but a model of the world of denotata with their general linguistic meaning" (Lotman 1977:37). Within such a literary reading there is by convention no pattern of formal coherence, e.g., symmetry or parallelism, that will be considered accidental.

The process of secondary semantization at work when an expression and its content create a second meaning is described by Lotman in a clear, if somewhat simplistic, manner:

> Thus the semantics of words in natural language are only raw material for the language of the artistic text. Drawn into superlinguistic structures, lexical units are like pronouns which derive their meaning from their correlation with the entire secondary system of semantic meanings. Words which are mutually isolated in the system of natural language prove to be functionally synonymous or antonymous when they occur in structurally equivalent positions. (Lotman 1977:170)

The use of form as a starting point for interpretation received a theoretical foundation in works like Lotman's, but it has much older roots. In fact, all hermeneutic schools in one way or another work on a similar foundation. Today many interpreters justify their works with arguments that fit into a semiotics of form. Fokkelman's book on *King David* (1981) makes an interesting case. He uses a semiotics of form as a heuristic tool, both positively and negatively. In his view formal patterns model the meaning of the biblical narrative, while at the same time they prevent hasty semantic conclusions.

One problematic aspect of this model is its lack of limitations. The infinity of possibilities for interpreting textual features as formally relevant and semantically meaningful is inherent in the basis of the model, which fails to provide any thorough reflection on perception and reading. Far-fetched readings are thus not prohibited. Critics seeking solutions to this problem have taken two directions. One is the positivistic search for "evidence" through the convergence of data. The more data pointing in the same direction, the more plausible the interpretation is.

This approach has two problems. One is the remaining weakness of evidence at all in interpretation. There is no way to tell the difference between random and meaningful form, between subjective and intersubjective features. Second, and more important, there is no connection between the impact of this sort of "evidence" and reading. The problem, then, remains the same: the interpretation may be considered arbitrary by its readers, however beautifully the evidence matches. The second course that critics have taken, primarily in Germany, is the "empirical" study of reception. Groeben (1977) provides an example. Those interpretations which most test-readers subscribe to are considered the best, that is, the most solidly grounded ones. The problem with this solution is, again, twofold. First, there is no protection against the banality that majority decisions entail. Second, the problem is only displaced onto another level. The readings of readers have to be read, and again, the metareadings can be distorting, far-fetched, or banal.

The only way, in my view, to deal with the lack of limitation is by applying the criteria of problem-solving. The existence of a problem has, then, to be posited first. This argument can be made on the basis of evidence from criticism. Once a problem is established, the plausibility within the interpretation as a whole and its relevance for the social background of the reader's community will have to make a case for the acceptance. In the case under consideration in this chapter, for example, the sophisticated analysis of the passage that frames the problematic line is not enough; the interpretation has to account for *both* the line and its problem.

The Use of Frame-Theory

The term *frame* was introduced long before Minski (1975) defined it as it is now used. It is borrowed from cognitive theory and has been applied to literature in several ways. One current definition can be found in Van Dijk (1977), where the term indicates a "set of propositions characterizing our conventional knowledge of some more or less autonomous situation (activity, course of events, state)."

In his elaboration of the concept for discourse analysis, Van Dijk (1977: 99) specifies that "such frames include propositions determining the possible ordering of facts." For the purpose of this chapter, it is important to note that convention is at stake. Frame-theory may have been further elaborated in recent years, but the use of the concept of frame in earlier, independent studies is not fundamentally different from the current one. Perry and Sternberg (1968; hereafter P&S), for example, in an article that is one of the cases under consideration here, do not explicitly refer to cognitive theory but nevertheless use the concept to indicate the conventional knowledge that forces readers to ask questions about unspecified circumstances in the text and to fill in the answers to those questions. Long before Iser's reader-response theory and Minski's frame-theory became fashionable, Perry and Sternberg integrated the idea of frame and the idea of gaps and gap-filling into a theory of the reading process, further elaborated in Perry (1979) and other publications, which they apply to the 2 Sam. 11 case.

In spite of differences between the theoretical basis of the concept and the practical use scholars make of it, all applications of the theory have in common the key idea that frames are conventional, implicit, and appropriate to be partially actualized, and that they help to construct normality. Normality may seem a shocking concept when applied to literature, since we are used to assuming that literature derives its value and aesthetic effect from its deviation from normality and convention. This may be true for much literature, but those deviations are possible only within the assumed coherence of the worlds involved in a fictional text, a coherence that depends heavily on a certain normality. In this respect, frames constitute an organizing principle. They organize knowledge about properties of objects and actions that typically belong together. It is this capacity to organize our perception of fictional worlds into typical sets of properties that makes us capable of coherently—and naturally—naturalizing "unnatural" worlds, e.g., of reading fiction and accepting it.

For Perry and Sternberg, as for many literary critics, frame-theory is used to provide a key to the filling of *gaps*. This is how cognitive theory is linked up with older aesthetic theories, like Wolfgang Kaiser's and, more recently, Iser's reader-response theory. Those theories attempt to give a basically affective theory a cognitive basis. "Gaps" are spots in the text where the information is insufficient, which provokes questions for the reader. It remains to be seen, however, to what extent the text "provokes"—in other words, how this personification of the text is used to cover a reader's response that cannot be accounted for outside the position of the reader as a subject. The problem is the same as the one Weber (1982) points out in Freud's texts about gaps. Perry and Sternberg's own missing of verse 21 will be shown to be a gap of precisely the type they try to pinpoint in the text. Not only do they miss the verse's characteristics, they also miss its status *as* gap, as informatively failing, that is. Hence, their reading turns out to be iconic of their own theory *and* its problems.

Perry and Sternberg connect gaps, and the use of frames to fill them, to the linearity of the text. Readers ask questions that will later be answered. If the question is never answered satisfactorily, the readers store their various answers and will maintain them as long as the answer is not given.

One consequence of the linear functioning of frames is their potentially conservative effect. When readers start with a specific question and this question is not answered, they may be hampered in their further reading, which becomes determined by their "obsession." This consequence is not theoretically stated; in Perry (1979) there is room for the abandoning of questions, and the author even states that questions need to be entertained. The application in P&S 1968 shows, however, that such a consequence is not excluded by the model (see "The Use of Frames," below).

A second heuristic problem is related to the theoretical status of gaps and frames. Perry (1979) claims an empirical status for gaps. He talks about the "systematic failure" of a text to give required information (39), about the "maximal concretization of the text that can be justified from the text itself" (43), and about the reader as "a metonymic characterization of the text" (43). For heuristic purposes, this argument poses the problem of the testability of gap-filling hypotheses. Since gaps are negatively defined (they are a *deficit*), there may arise a problem of relevance: how general and how generally relevant are the questions one particular interpreter may ask? This drawback makes the negatively defined concept less suited to meet the negative criterion defined above.

This problem is important for our present purpose. Perry (1979) gives a sophisticated set of criteria for evaluating the use of frames for gap-filling. The best frames meet the criteria of linking the highest number of disparate items and connecting them most closely—two requirements that are based on the convention of *unity*. In the case under consideration, this convention pushes interpreters toward "explaining-away" activities, and I will show that the procedure is not satisfactory. The third criterion is based on convention in general: the frame that is the most typical or conventional is the best. Perry says that this is the most problematic criterion, but he does not discuss how its adoption may influence the practice of reading. The interpretation may entirely rest on it. Since convention is an unavoidable but nevertheless conservative force, it also leads to the naturalization of problematic features in the text: of gaps.

This point leads to my most basic objection to the common use of frame-theory as a hermeneutic model. Convention is a strong force and we cannot do without it. But it becomes tricky as soon as frames are assumed to be unbreakable, and when gap-filling is designed to restore the menaced frames. Thus the concept of frames leads to the justification of interpretations that can be as far-fetched as they want. For there is no standard for the relevance of the "nonexisting" gaps. The use of frames for the naturalization of unargued gaps is at the same time based on the blurring of suspect difficulties. This conservative use is not inherent in the concept and the theory behind it, but the theory does nothing to prevent it. It rather encourages it by stating the basic vagueness and implicitness of frames.

The Use of Narratology

Narratology has been generally applied to narrative texts since the early days of structuralism. It started as an attempt to generalize as abstractly as possible about the narrative genre, and applications were initially meant as tests for the general theory (see, for example, "classics" like Bremond 1972 and Greimas 1965, 1970, but also Hendricks 1973). Soon scholars got tired of the irrelevance of mere formulae and tables for the study of literature, and at the same time it proved impossible to discard interpretation altogether and thus reach perfect generalization. So the efforts shifted from positing generalizable structures to proposing heuristically useful models. An important contribution of narratology to the study of literature lies, in my opinion, in this heuristic use. It allows one to connect a specific interpretation with the particular semiotic strategies of a text.

Drama has a basic, though only technical, democratic structure; in narrative, the origins of meaning, and hence meaning itself, are hidden in its seemingly monological structure (one text, one speaker). Within the framework of this overall monological structure, however, the textual subjectivity is problematic. According to both philosophical accounts (see, for example, Coward and Ellis 1977) and commonly used dictionaries, modern Western society uses a highly confused, inconsistent concept of the subject, which needs to be taken into full account if we want to grasp its impact on social life. Attempting to undo the concept of its synonymy with the human individual, while preserving its various aspects in common use, one could try to define the semiotic subject as *the support of semiotic action, the starting point of its pragmatic dimension and the center of its semantic dimension, which combines, produces, conveys, represses, and retains meanings according to the rules of the systems in which it functions* (for an extensive argument in support of this definition, see Bal 1986). Subjects in this already complex sense play a major part in narrative subjectivity. Since manipulation of meaning enhances ideological influence, the analysis of this process, especially in the case of the socially dominant narrative practice, is highly relevant (see, for example, Jameson 1981).

For the analysis of narrative subjectivity, the narratological distinction between narrator, focalizer, and agent, that is, between the subjects of speech, vision, and action, hierarchically related, is a first, useful, though still very coarse one (for a detailed presentation, see Bal 1985). Narratology as a hermeneutic model (see also Genette's basic study, 1972) can make good use of these concepts and the distinctions they are based on. The simple questions: Who speaks? Who "sees"? Who acts? when applied to a specific text may either provide direct answers, and thus show the structure of meaning in its pragmatic dimension, or else prove to be problematic. In the latter case, the text's subjectivity is problematic, and consequently, its ideological impact is blurred. These cases are interesting for several reasons. Through their problematic structure, they demonstrate the way in which the subject and its assumed unity were problematized, though most probably unconsciously, by the author and his or her social environment. Second, the reception of such texts shows a tendency toward naturalization, that is, a tendency to solve the problems and interpret the text in a unifying, reassuringly "natural" way. It is quite possible that the convention of unity, so powerful in our history of criticism, is seductive because of its potential to keep the disturbing uncertainty of the subject buried. That it functions in precisely this way, and that gender politics stimulates it, will be substantiated throughout this book.

Compared to the two previously discussed models, this one has the advantage on the one hand of being genre-bound, which allows specification (surplus requirement), and, on the other, of being generalizable beyond the narrow field of literature to other semiotic practices. Or, to put it differently: it contributes to a fuller understanding of the text and its effect while at the same time deepening our insight into the semiotic particularities of narrative as a specific discursive practice. This insight can help us, beyond literature, to understand the use we make of narrative in social life. These two possible extensions implied in the model enlarge the relevance of the interpretations it helps to formulate.

The Use of the Text

Now that the theoretical assumptions underlying the three models are mapped out, we will, in the following sections, look at the way the models are used to support, articulate, or generate interpretations. Special focus on the detail of verse 21 is meant to bring problems to the fore that are not obvious at first sight. In order to make my case as convincing as possible, I will give the sample readings more of the benefit of the doubt than I would do were my goal different. I will accept their assumptions, that is, and look at how they work within the framework of the critical enterprises themselves.

Faithful to their theoretical frameworks, Perry and Sternberg and Fokkelman start with questions derived from them. Thus they avoid making

hasty interpretations and jumping to moral conclusions. Their interpretations are literary, not theological. Perry and Sternberg soon come to
a question the reader is supposed to ask, that is, does Uriah know that
David has slept with his wife, that she is pregnant, and that he has been
called back in order to cover this up? Fokkelman begins with an examination of the formal structure of the text, paying close attention to such
figures as chiasmus, parallelism, and concentric construction. Perry and
Sternberg discuss the initial question as one of linearity. Fokkelman deals
with the text as we usually deal with poetry, that is, without taking the
linear unfolding into account. Both analyses are minutely detailed and
subtle. Consequently, there is no important adequacy problem: readers
of these interpretations will feel that the text as it stands is extensively
dealt with. As for plausibility, one problematic side of the standard has to
be stressed beforehand. Plausibility must be confronted with the surplus
requirement. As is shown in recent empirical reception-studies (Groeben
1977), plausibility tends to favor the most banal interpretation. And it
favors conservatism, in that it does not encourage frame-breaking. On
the other hand, plausibility is best tested when the interpretation is confronted with a textual problem and a textual characteristic. The provocation a textual problem represents makes naturalization difficult, so that
the question of plausibility is brought to the fore. Relevance is subject-
dependent, and has to be subdivided according to the themes it reinforces. Conservation versus frame-breaking is one theme, which may
be completed by considerations concerning the position of women, since
woman-man relations seem to be an issue in this text.

The textual problem already referred to—"Who smote Abimelech the
Son of Jerubbesheth? did not a woman cast a piece of a millstone upon
him from the wall, that he died in Thebez?"—is recognized by both
interpretations as a problem. It is part of an instruction given by Joab to
a messenger. It is supposed to be an anticipated angry reaction by David
when he learns about the losses his army suffered in the execution of the
murder of Uriah. The problem is that the example of Abimelech seems
doubly irrelevant. Nobody has been killed by a woman in the present
case, and David has little reason to be angry. It looks like a confusion of
subjects, a confusion that is reflected on the formal level by the compli-
cated figure of embedding: Joab says to the messenger that David will say
something, and this quote is embedded in turn in the narrator's discourse.

The text can be globally characterized by two features: a negative one
and a positive one. There is a total absence of inner views, narrator's
comments, and motivation of actions. Consequently, there is a difficulty
for those readers who want to understand why the king did what he did.
This burden creates a moral problem. Perry and Sternberg refer to this

stylistic characteristic as irony, because it creates a gap between the seriousness of the events and the dry tone in which they are narrated. This is a better solution than the one chosen by Scholes and Kellog (1966: 166–67), who consider it a feature of primitivism, an ideologically suspect view of literary evolution. Irony is a concept, however, that goes too easily with all sorts of phenomena, and, as a synonym for or explanation of ambiguity, it is not exclusive enough to be a useful tool. In the present case, it prevents the reader from making more specific interpretations. One such interpretation could be based on the psychoanalytic concept of repression. The lack of evaluation could, then, be conceived as an iconic sign of the lack of clarity that all the subjects involved feel about the precise location of responsibility.

One positive characteristic of the text is the symmetry in the structure of events. In 1–13, the adultery plus the attempt at concealment is presented; in 15–27, the murder plus the attempt at its concealment. This arrangement establishes a parallel between sex and violence and makes 14 the pivot of the text. The interpretation of 14 is not a textual problem, since its integration is not particularly problematic, but it does nevertheless provide another center of interest (as it is the center of the text). I will therefore concentrate the discussion on its centrality.

The Use of Symmetry

Fokkelman's interpretation rests heavily on a minute stylistic study of the text, its metrical and phonological form and the structuring principles of its immediate content, considered in turn as a set of signs. The interpreter is extremely sensitive to figures like chiasmus and parallelism, repetition of sounds and of meanings. In this, he makes an astute use of what he claims to be the implicit poetics of the Bible, in which these figures play an important role under the perhaps too general heading of parallelism (see Kugel 1981). The approach is semiotic in that it treats the features of natural language as well as semantic elements as secondary signs.

One of the many examples of secondary semantization is the spatial opposition that underlies the text. David's staying in Jerusalem, where he is idle and thus ready for mischief, obviously contrasts with the army's hard life at the front, represented by Joab and, problematically, by Uriah. Within the city, the palace and its elevated roof, whence the king perceives Bathsheba, contrasts with the house of the couple, where Bathsheba is focalized. Between the open field and the city walls at the front, there is another spatial opposition. In each case, the border between the two opposites is transgressed, a transgression that constitutes an event in

Lotman's sense: "An event in a text is the shifting of a persona across the borders of a semantic field" (Lotman 1977:233). On the basis of Fokkelman's analysis, one may consider as events in this specific sense: the adultery that connects the palace and the house, Uriah's remaining in the court of the palace instead of going home to his wife (a negative event), his bringing the letter containing his death sentence from the city to the front, the soldiers (Uriah being one) coming too close to the walls of the city, the message delivered to David from the front, and David's bringing Bathsheba into the palace for matrimony.

Fokkelman analyzes what he calls the "chiasmus of distance," a repeated figure that stresses both the opposition and its transgression, and interprets it as a sign of the interest those in power have in the maintenance of the strict social order, which is symbolized spatially. Refusing to stay within the spatial position assigned to him, Uriah signs his own death sentence: "Having come from far away, Uriah must disappear again never to return home" (57).

The most interesting part of this interpretation, in my view, is the section devoted to the second half of the text, 14–27. Fokkelman studies the different figures of symmetry within this part and plausibly assigns meaning to them. However, by the simple fact that he starts a new paragraph here, Fokkelman stresses less the symmetry within 1–27 than the subsymmetry within 14–27 (he integrates both parts later, pp. 92–96). There is an interesting consequence to this emphasis: the center of the overall symmetry, 14, is not considered as such, but the center of the second half is 21, the verse containing the textual problem. Within the concentric structure of 14–27, the instruction by Joab to the messenger is central, and within it, the incoherent line on Abimelech's death. This central place for a nonevent that, quantitatively speaking, seems equally overrated is, within the semiotics of form, a definite sign. Its reality status is problematic on different levels. Doubly embedded, it is doubly fictive, since the narrator quotes the character Joab within a fictional tale, while Joab quotes a speech of his own invention, attributed (Prince 1982) to David but never delivered by him. This (later falsified) prediction of David's anger is explained by Fokkelman within the framework of Gestalt psychology as a catastrophic expectation, which tells us more about the character who is entertaining the expectation than about the one who is supposed to fulfill the expectation. Thus the interpretation shifts from David to Joab. Fokkelman sees in this pessimism a projection of Joab's own anger and guilt, since he feels the king has misused him, forced him to deploy bad strategy and murder a good soldier. Bringing up Abimelech's death, Joab unconsciously shows that he feels that a woman is involved, and that David's part is not an honorable one.

This interpretation of the textual problem is interesting and convincing. It renders justice to the problematic side of the problem, and thus avoids the seductiveness of the explaining-away strategy. It does not fully explain, however, a few details, the relevance of which, it is true, is not self-evident and will be demonstrated later. The comparison between the tyrant Abimelech and David is not a flattering one. But, technically speaking, David is not the one compared: it was the innocent Uriah, among other soldiers, who was neither a tyrant nor a king, whose death resembled Abimelech's. There is confusion of both subjects of speech and objects and subjects of action, and, moreover, of moral value: so much confusion needs, perhaps, to be further accounted for. The most interesting problem of the verse, the meaning of the woman within this male context of war, and one that may be the main connective between 1–14 and 15–27, is only partially explained. Joab senses the involvement of a woman, indeed, but the sentence specifies more than can thus be accounted for. Within the comparison the woman means danger, death. Fokkelman suggests the following series of motifs of the comparison: death, woman, wall, battle, shame, folly. He rightly states that a real comparison between the two cases falls flat (69). The falling flat of the comparison is described, but not explained in itself. The comparison equates murderer and victim, and that is surprising enough, but it may also be asked why it is that the danger the woman represents in this comparison brings this equation about. It needs a reflection on the status of the subject in order to interpret the paradox that what was initially the object of focalization and lust is turned in verse 21 into the powerful subject that decides over life and death.

For the moment, it seems justifiable to conclude that Fokkelman does offer a plausible and adequate interpretation of the textual problem, which borrows its relevance from the framework of Gestalt psychology. As such, it gives insight into the human psyche, it explains how people handle problems that are too burdensome for them, and it may thus contribute to diluting excessive anxiety in the reader's life. Nevertheless, it leaves the problems it so carefully describes partially unexplained. Those are problems concerning the status of the subject, the view of woman expressed, and the distribution of power.

Full justice is done to the obvious and the hidden symmetry, and this analysis may even be considered exemplary in its completeness in this respect. The option for a division into two separate paragraphs, however, slightly blurs the symmetry between the two scenes, the mutual equivalence of sex and violence it implies, and the central place of the letter in 14. The negative characteristic of the text, its lack of inner views and narratorial comment, is not elaborated.

The Use of Frames

Perry and Sternberg present, in an equally extensive analysis of the text, an interpretation that is less based on form, though they do take formal features into account. The difference is nonetheless basic, for the structuring function of the formal principle is replaced here by the guiding function of the so-called gaps. Formal phenomena are included incidentally, more as extra evidence than as one coherent structure. The gap-filling by the reader, it is argued, is hampered by the impossibility of deciding in favor of one hypothesis rather than another on the basis of textual evidence. To the question, Does Uriah know what is happening? the two possible answers are equally likely and equally problematic. Thus the reader constantly shifts from one hypothesis to the other, a movement that enhances an artistic effect of ambiguity (see also Rimmon 1977). This ambiguity also leads to two different views of the characters of both Uriah and David. If Uriah knows, then his too perfect idealism in his refusal to go home is balanced by strategy, and he thus becomes more "round" (Forster 1954). The same character would be more "flat" as a sheer idealist. A David who assumes that Uriah knows would be a dark, plotting criminal, while in the opposite case, his uncertainty would make him more "round." This artistic argument in favor of one hypothesis is but one of many arguments the authors advance, and indeed we may agree with their conclusion that a decision is impossible.

Perry and Sternberg devote an extensive paragraph to the textual problem. Insisting on the disordered and disproportionate style of Joab's anticipation of David's speech, they too are sensitive to its exceptional character. The style is explained as an imitation of the emotional reaction expected of David. The reference to Abimelech as a "classic" of military bad luck is easily naturalized in this interpretation. According to Perry and Sternberg, the analogy between the two cases is based on the situational details: soldiers coming too close to a wall and as a result suffering losses. This motif of analogy is explicitly mentioned. For that reason, Perry and Sternberg call this a close analogy. In such a case, however, other aspects may remain open. Those uncontrolled aspects are in this case: the status of the fallen besieger (king vs. commoner), the identity and sex of the killer (woman vs. soldier), and the place of action (Thebez vs. Rabbah). The differences between both sides of the analogy are explained within the broader, figurative meaning: David, like Abimelech, falls, though morally, because of a woman. In this interpretation, the two parts of the text are brought into contact by a double metaphor: David has fallen into moral disgrace by the doings of a woman as Abimelech has literally fallen by the physical actions of a woman. In another sense, Uriah metaphorically equals Abimelech: he too falls—literally, by the hand of a person on the wall, though male, *and* figuratively, through the "doings" of his wife. Implicit in the first metaphor is a negative view of David, for Abimelech, a tyrant, at least went to the war, while David, Israel's most venerated king, was led to his base deed through idleness. Implicit in the second metaphor, in this interpretation, is the guilt that falls to the woman.

Unlike Fokkelman, Perry and Sternberg do not shift their attention from David to Joab. David remains the chief character, and therefore they pay little attention to the possibility that the comparison concerns Uriah rather than David. Like Fokkelman, they are aware of the problematic details in the comparison. Their interpretation is not based on psychology. It partly leaves open what is open, and thus they manage to avoid the explaining-away strategy. On the other hand, they integrate the passage into an overall unity by labeling the inconsistencies as irony and, more surprisingly, by laying much of the responsibility on the woman. The inconsistent male subject (is David or Uriah the compared? Is the messenger or David the addressee?) is then balanced by a consistent female subject, bringing death in battle and shame in bed by the same move. Thus, they partly account for the relations between the two parts of the text, but they seem unaware of the implications of their interpretation. Insistently speaking of "Bathsheba's infidelity" (e.g., 201–204), referring to Uriah as a possible "cuckold," they betray an ideological position about love that deserves further examination and that may properly be called a *frame* (kept implicit this time).

Their interpretation pays close attention to the negative characteristic of the text, while the positive one (symmetry) is less accounted for. They deal explicitly with the textual problem, but the relevance of their interpretation of it seems doubtful to me. It gives no specific insight into psychological or social motivations, which, as I shall argue shortly, are highly important in this case. But, significantly for my argument, they also simplify the textual structure.

The most problematic aspect of this analysis is its relevance. The initial question, "Does Uriah know?" does not impose itself upon the reader at all. In their concluding section, they compare the case with James's *The Turn of the Screw*. The difference that makes the comparison fall flat is, however, double. In James's story, the ambiguity (does the ghost "exist" or is it the result of the governess's imagination?) is thematized explicitly in the text. This is not the case here. Moreover, each option the reader may choose implies a specific genre: he or she opts for the fantastic if the ghost is assumed to exist or for psychological literature if it is not. This is not the case here either.

It is curious that in such an extensive article, in which hardly anything is left implicit, the reasons why this particular question is supposed to have general relevance are not once addressed. An explanation may be attempted: only within a specific ideology of love, in which woman is man's property and adultery is automatically blamed on the woman, will a question of this kind be accepted by their readers as plausible. Characteristically, Fokkelman, who never blames Bathsheba and who, on the contrary, describes her as a victim whose interests are not taken into account, never considers the question that is so basic for Perry and Sternberg's approach. Anxiety about possible adultery seems to go against respect for the victimized woman.

Both interpretations are, it deserves to be stressed, interesting and refined; they offer a more profound and sophisticated interpretation than the average reader can perform and thus meet the standard of surplus information. They are adequate enough, within the framework of their initial questions. Fokkelman's model of formal patterns offers more guarantees for plausibility, though in practice Perry and Sternberg also do justice to form, even if their model does not call for it. Positively, both models, at least in their samples, offer heuristic tools that can lead to good interpretations. Negatively, and this is important, the semiotics of form does prevent irrelevant interpretative statements, while frame-theory does not.

The Use of the Subject

As soon as one examines the tale in terms of narratological categories, the latter turn out to be strikingly thematized. One example of each category suffices to demonstrate the relevance of an initial examination of narrative subjects.

Speech. David's speeches in which he tells Uriah to go home and join his wife (8, 10) thematize a conception of language strongly anchored in a particular structure of power. The pragmatic goal of the speeches is misunderstood by the addressee, who does not take the particular "felicity conditions" into account. By thus failing to get the intended message he proves to be basically subversive. What David meant as an order is taken as an offer that can be either accepted or rejected. Uriah believes in his own freedom of choice, while David, like the chiefs in the film *The Godfather*, thinks he has made "an offer he can't refuse." More than an instrument for the communication of opinions, advice, and decisions, discourse flagrantly betrays its place in a social structure of inequality as a monologic, manipulative practice. David's power is exercised exclusively by means of discourse, not action. His idleness is stressed (1) and his discursive activity is quantitatively important (8, 10, 12, 15, 25). Except for the failed dialogue with Uriah, all of David's speech is monologic.

Because of this exclusive use of discourse, it tends to represent an abuse of language.

Focalization. David as the focalizer of Bathsheba's beauty (2) is immediately influenced by his vision. To see her is, for a man in his position, to possess her. Here, too, the narrative activity is strongly emphasized in a thematic development. As such, it is later reversed in the textually problematic passage (21). While in verse 2 the woman is the object of the higher-placed focalizer, the position is reversed in 21, which alludes to the woman who, in Judg. 9:53, is the higher-placed female and who kills the lower-placed male victim, Abimelech—like David, a king. The higher-lower opposition in this motif symbolizes the inequality of power, which is implied in unilateral focalization as it is in unilateral discourse. Reduced to a passive object, Bathsheba is victimized in 2 as Abimelech is in 21, as evoked by Joab-David. This reversal is, of course, as yet unexplained. It needs explanation, since the reversal of power is not only illogical in relation to the other events in the fabula but also embedded in the speech by Joab-David.

Action. David is, within an actantial analysis, the subject of action. His lust sets the action in motion, and, with the help of his servants (obligatory, not freely offered help), his power decides the positive fulfillment of his narrative program: to possess Bathsheba (2–4). Significantly, there are no opponents. But a program so utterly successful is narratively uninteresting: the resulting fabula is too short. Hence, in a next phase, a new program has to be more difficult to fulfill. The second phase is set in motion as a consequence of the first, that is, by Bathsheba's pregnancy. The goal is concealment, and again David's absolute power is invested with the feature of a positive *destinateur*. This time, however, there is an opponent: Uriah. How can this "servant of the king" make the mighty David nearly fail as a narrative subject? Powerless, he can only negatively (that is, by refusal) provoke David's own weakness as an agent. David's action itself is negative. His only activity consists of avoiding his responsibilities. The pregnancy and the subsequent murder are to be displaced onto others, Uriah and Joab. Power makes its objects passive, since the powerful use other agents as instruments. In all his absolute power, David is basically passive. The superman of verse 4 comes to resemble a non-man in the rest of the fabula.

As a subject of speech and focalization, David seems strong because he is powerful, but he is, in fact, weak because these semiotic activities are used for noncommunicative purposes. As an agent, he works hard to absent himself, leaving the handling of his problems to others. This displacement points to a fundamental metonymy, which reveals, like a return of the repressed, a problematic subjectivity, betrayed with particular acuity in verse 21.

Before we can turn to the textual problem itself, Uriah's position still has to be clarified. In verse 14, David sends Uriah back to the front with a letter that condemns him to death. Coming between the two parts of the tale, the story of the adultery plus its attempted concealment, and the story of the murder plus its attempted concealment, this event is a crucial one. The letter contains the order to Joab to make Uriah die as a victim of an act of *desolidarity*: the soldiers are to retire and leave him alone at a dangerous spot. We recall that Uriah refused to go home and join his wife out of solidarity with his comrades at the front (11). Obviously, solidarity is an issue in this tale. This particular death sentence is not only the elimination of an embarrassing opponent but also a specific punishment for a specific crime.

If we consider narratological categories such as speech and speakers, vision and focalizers, action and actors, as well as, within the level of the fabula, space, events, and situations, the letter constitutes a transition with respect to all of them.

Speech. The letter is the only written discourse and, as such, is a transition between narratorial report and actorial speech.

Speakers. David speaks in the letter, but he needs Uriah's collaboration for the letter to reach its addressee, so that there is a "combined speaker."

Focalization. No particular limitation of view can be assumed here. The facts are reported in the absence of any possible focalizer.

Focalizers. Hence, there is no actorial focalizer, since David, who knows the content of the letter, is absent, Joab, not yet present, and Uriah, unaware of the content of the letter.

Action. There is no action like crime or concealment of crime involved here, no sex and no violence. The passage is the short transition between the two stages of the fabula, symmetrically arranged.

Agents. This is the only passage where a single agent performs the action. In the first part, David deals with Bathsheba, his servants, and Uriah. In the second part, Joab deals with his soldiers, his messenger, and (indirectly) David. Here—and here only—Uriah acts alone.

Events. This passage is a transition between the two programs of concealment and the two semantic fields that set those programs in motion: sex and violence. It is also the transition between the two strategies, persuasion versus force. Third, it is a transition between David's two appeals to his men's solidarity and collaboration, first addressed to Uriah, then to Joab.

Space. Between the city and the front, between maximum safety and comfort and ultimate danger, Uriah is spatially free. Between the two groups in opposition, the idlers (female domain) and the soldiers (male domain), he is in a no-man's land.

Situation. Between the reassuringly clear positions of the husband and the soldier, both belonging to a group, Uriah is here isolated. Between secrecy and publicness, Uriah carries the sealed but written, and hence potentially public, secret of David's crime.

Text. It is not surprising that the verse that reports this event, central in all possible senses but especially in Lotman's, is placed at the very center of the tale: verse 14, of 27 verses.

What can be the meaning of this transitory function of Uriah's only solitary action? It is ironic that the passage in which Uriah functions as a mediator, the passage that is, in the narratological and the semantic sense, mediation itself, contains the event in which mediation is used to shut out the mediator from all human contact and to prepare for him a death of absolute isolation.

This paradox is also striking in the analysis of Uriah's positions in this passage. Some of these positions point to a positive transition, others to a negative one: sometimes Uriah is in a position of *mediation,* connecting both parts of the text and the semantic fields involved, sometimes he is in a position of *separation,* radically disconnecting them. Beyond conscious strategy, Uriah's guilt, in David's unconscious view, must be a heavy one.

Uriah's proclaimed solidarity with his comrades, in verse 11, must have been particularly painful to David for several reasons. Obviously this good soldier holds a mirror up to David, showing him what real solidarity is and how much the king lacks it. Uriah's is a positive solidarity, sharing pain, hardship, and danger. Confronting it is painful to the king not only because of the implied criticism of his idle and comfortable life at the palace, which so sharply contrasts with the hard life the soldiers live for his sake. It is even more so because David appeals to another solidarity: the collaboration demanded by the man in trouble "because of" a woman. David had the intention of enjoying love "the male way," that is, for brief satisfaction, without consequences. What must make him feel humiliated is that Bathsheba's pregnancy and Uriah's refusal to take over David's responsibility for it impose on him, the powerful king, the "female" rhythm of love: he is stuck with a child. Uriah is, in fact, and probably without being aware of it (whether he is or not *is* irrelevant; what is asked of him remains the same), asked to help David out of that painful position. In refusing this negative male solidarity, Uriah in fact excludes himself from the ideological community to which he belongs. His punctiliousness, his decency in this respect, his view of what is "proper" as expressed in his discourse stating what real solidarity is, as opposed to the negative solidarity David claims, is maintained throughout David's repeated attempts to pull him back into his group—by making him drink, for example. In the end it is answered by David's punctiliousness in excluding him altogether. Thus the particular death David chooses for him is more than just practical strategy: it is *vendetta.*

It is not surprising that Joab, unaware of what has happened, misses precisely that point in the instruction, and carries it out differently. He thus takes over the narrative program, creating a prolonging effect since in consequence the course of events needs further development, e.g., the speech containing the textual problem. Joab takes David's place as the actantial subject, and as such he obeys the law of male solidarity as David seemed to understand it. Only within such an *esprit de corps* (!) can actors be mutually substituted. In the discussion of the textual problem, the extent to which this substitution may be a logical consequence of a shared unconscious attitude will become clearer.

The textual problem, the strangely illogical rhetorical question in verse 21, is framed by two logically contradictory statements within the same speech, Joab's instruction to the messenger. This frame is in itself a (minor) textual problem.

> 19: "When thou hast made an end of telling all the matters of
> the war unto the king,"
> 21: "... then say thou, Thy servant Uriah the Hittite is dead
> also."

Only when one is aware of what happened in 1–13 is it possible to distinguish *all* the matters of the war from Uriah's death. For "officially," that is, according to Joab's conscious knowledge, Uriah died a soldier's death.

In both of the interpretations discussed, this logical inconsistency is noted. The relation between the two parts of this frame can be described in rhetorical terms, and then it belongs to different figures of speech. It can be decomposed (see Chase 1986 for this term of "new rhetoric") as follows:

Synecdoche: Uriah's death is part of all the matters of the war.

Equivalence: Uriah's death is equally important for all the matters of the war.

Metaphor: "All the matters of the war" is the *comparant* of Uriah's death, as the social is of the individual, as war is of love—a significant metaphor.

Antithesis: The negative result of the war is opposed to the positive result represented by Uriah's death.

No relation: Uriah's death is a *corpus alienum* (Fokkelman 1981:85) among the matters of the war, as the framed rhetorical question is among Joab's utterances.

The different possible meanings that come to light in this way are certainly not mutually exclusive. If we are to decompose the figure, they must all be retained to make us fully aware of the confusion of which this passage is a symptom and that is embedded in a speech delivered by a man who cannot have any factual knowledge of what Uriah's death means to the king. This confusion cannot but rest on a deep intuitive identification between the two powerful men, the king and his stand-in at the front.

It is only when we assume such an intuitive identification, based on the common interest men have when facing women, that we can fully understand, and fully decompose, the inconsistency of the rhetorical question.

As Fokkelman specifies (69, n. 19), the comparison between Abimelech's death and what happened at the front, falling flat as it seems to do, rests on six motifs: death-woman-wall-battle-shame-folly. This curious series deserves further examination. Strangely, the most problematic motif (there is no woman involved in the Uriah case) is explicitly mentioned in the text (21: "did not a woman cast a piece of a millstone upon him from the wall?"). We can assume with Fokkelman, therefore, that in Joab's intuitive view there is a woman involved here, too.

The differences between the described situations are even more numerous than the analogies. They can be outlined as follows:

20: They *shoot* from the wall—aggressive and professional, male competence
21: She *throws* from the wall—passive and amateurish, female (in-?)competence
20: Collective subject—major danger
21: Individual subject—minor danger?
20: Male subject
21: Female subject
20: Collective object—fallen because of Joab's partially failing understanding
21: Individual object—fallen because of the victim's failing understanding
20: Noble object—soldiers in the king's service
21: Abject object—a usurper
20: Arrows—appropriate instrument of war
21: Millstone—inappropriate, instrument of peace

These oppositions are clearly systematic and must therefore be confronted with the similarities, which they put into a particular perspective.

The similarities listed by Fokkelman—death, woman, wall, battle, shame, folly—can now easily be interpreted within the psychoanalytical framework. They express the unconscious complex of the fear of woman, and can be understood to say something like this: one dies a shameful death as soon as one is so foolish as to fight woman when she is defending her wall/entrance from her mighty position as the feared other. Such a confession, so shameful in itself, needs, of course, to be firmly censored. The differences listed above constitute one form of this censorship. But, as a return of the repressed, the systematic oppositional character of that list betrays the hidden reinforcement of the obvious analogy as shown by Fokkelman's list.

Once we assume that the evocation of Abimelech's death has something to do with such an unconscious fear of women, we can return to the narratological problem of the speaker, which forms the second form of censorship in the displacement of the subject. As we have seen, the enigmatic sentence lies within a complex figure of fictional embedding. That figure is so complex that sophisticated readers like Perry and Sternberg become trapped. They interpret the passage as a subtle hint to David, whom Joab wants to criticize without the knowledge of his messenger. This reading is inconsistent with the narrative structure, since the sentence is part of Joab's speech to the messenger and not of what the messenger has to tell David. Such a mistake, however, can in this case hardly be blamed on the interpreters. For it demonstrates how easily one confuses the parties involved, and the likeliness of that confusion is, in my view, the basic message of this passage. That is the first reason for my objection to Fokkelman's otherwise plausible interpretation of the sentence as a project of Joab, who is thus supposed to express his unconscious anger and guilt feelings. This interpretation takes the text carefully "at its words" but does not take into account the very complexity of its narratological structure as an expression of its semantic incoherence. The second, related reason, is the ideology of individualism it entails. Blaming David, it whitewashes Joab and gets away with individual guilt where social structure is at stake. I favor an interpretation that accounts for both the precise structure and the mistakes it provokes: only then can one claim to connect interpretation to reading and effect of texts.

The displacement inherent in this sentence concerns the speaker as well as the spoken of. The metaphorical evocation of Abimelech has two compared objects: David and Uriah. Literally, Uriah is the victim compared to Abimelech. He died in the circumstances listed by Fokkelman: being too near the wall, he got shot from the wall. Figuratively, too, he is the compared object in one sense: he had to die because of a woman. Metonymically, the compared object is, however, displaced onto David. Like Abimelech, he is a usurper of what does not belong to him. And he, too, is in danger because of a woman: stuck with child, covered with shame. Again, two men are interchanged.

Joab may feel angry with David and guilty about Uriah, as Fokkelman puts it. But he speaks here "in David's name," imagining David's obsession to an unnamed messenger. His anger is displaced in its turn: let us not forget that in his evocation, the woman is the killer. It is possible that his anger with David about the bad strategy and the death of an innocent man imposed on him, an anger that, as a subordinate "servant of the king," he cannot afford, is directed against the intuitively appropriate scapegoat, woman in general.

The confusion noticed in all these different levels of meaning is the consequence of an ambiguity in David's messages. In this respect, both parts of the text are profoundly symmetrical. In 8, David sends Uriah home, but he does not name the real destination: the woman. In 15, the content of the letter does not specify the reason for Uriah's death: the woman. In both cases, the addressed other man has to complete the message himself. David does not specify the location of his interest. In 11, Uriah names the woman, in 21, Joab names her. As we saw already at a first narratological questioning of the text, David speaks only partially. Pragmatically, the utterances in 8 and 15 are unilateral orders, not communicative dialogue. Semantically, they contain only half of the information. In both cases, the other man is asked for help, at his own expense: Uriah is either stuck with another man's child or killed, and Joab has bad strategy imposed on him. The solidarity of the victim is required, not only in factual action but also in *naming the woman*. David, as a subject, is so weak that he needs others to speak his mind. Uriah ultimately refuses to stand with the men against the woman; he wants to stand with the men only in positive, not in negative, solidarity. This conviction is, in my view, the underlying reason for his death and for the ambiguous transitory function he fulfills in 14. Joab, as opposed to Uriah, does not refuse. He stands with David against the woman, he justifies the attitude of both by evoking the danger she represents, and, in spite of uncomfortable feelings about it, he is ready to execute the "traitor," Uriah.

The Use of Competition

The preceding exercise in comparative hermeneutics was meant to prepare the ground for the following chapters. It seems useful to reassess the point of the comparison, the competition it entails, and the theoretical digressions it necessitated. The interpretations have been presented as representative of the practice of literary criticism of the Bible today. The analysis of their assumptions and of the guidelines the critics have followed showed both the importance and the limits of theoretical models for hermeneutic performance. At the crucial moment, when the textual problem came up, the models failed the critics, because the critics already knew what was relevant. This does not mean that the model is then irrelevant. Its use changes: instead of directing the interpretation, it supports it; not the model but the critics' preconceptions inform the interpretation. The model, with all the authority of academic conventions, allows the critics to give their views a status they do not deserve.

The academic authority inherent in scholarly interpretations allows for the relevance of the competition between them that this chapter has staged. Within the academic practice that is at stake here, the most accepted way to argue for or against interpretations is to show that one is "better" than the other, either for its own sake or because of the more acceptable model it rests on. Application of the criteria discussed can be helpful for such a comparative evaluation. The painstaking effort to argue the whole way, from the basic question of the use of models, via the brief examination of the selected models, to the evaluation of the interpretation, was a conscious attempt to discuss within the critics' own framework.

The detail that has guided the discussion throughout was selected for its manifold aspects. As a case of figurative language, an intertextual metaphor, it is an extremely sophisticated piece of literature. Embedded in a complex and, in its very complexity, problematic narrative structure, it is also an extremely sophisticated narrative unit. As an example as well of an extremely complex confusion of gender relations, it makes a case for a problematic of representation as related to gender. All this speculation would still have been of limited relevance if it were not for the response it gave rise to. The real issue of the discussion was not the text but the critics. The practice of criticism as used for the imposition, under the cover of academic authority, of gender-specific interests is what my analysis ultimately was meant to bring to the fore.

The analysis illustrates one more point that, raised in the preface to this book, needs constant enhancing: the quality of dominance. The two interpretations, both biased in some way, have been shown to be different, not only in method, but also in ideology. The one based on frame-theory is, in my view, more grossly sexist, while the other one is very subtly and indirectly so. It is through the mediation of liberalism and individualism that Fokkelman's interpretation blames one man, thus exonerating the other; by doing this, he eliminates the most painful sting of patriarchy: the solidarity *against* the other. Typically, and not by coincidence, it is the former reading that makes blunt mistakes, while the latter, more careful, neatly untangles the confusion. This is "progress of knowledge," but at the same time, a more subtle form of bias. Eliminating the textual problem, Fokkelman eliminates the social problem, making it merely an individual matter. It is only when the problem is both enhanced and interpreted *as a problem* that we can hope to explain more than the text alone. For the problem is, and must be shown as such, a *sextual* problem.

· 2 ·

DELILAH DECOMPOSED:
SAMSON'S TALKING CURE AND
THE RHETORIC OF SUBJECTIVITY

Reading Heroes

The articulation of interpretations on the basis of the narratological model of subjectivity: such was the argument of the preceding chapter. In this chapter, that proposal will be further explored. The procedure starts with the routine whodunit questions: who speaks, who focalizes, who acts? The aim is not so much to receive an answer but to reveal crucial problems in the text: of genre, of representation, and again, of textual detail. Leaving the questions unanswered will allow us to point out textual elements that seem problematic. The confrontation with reception documents confirms the problematic status of the details that the model fails to accommodate. Thus, the model just put into place is immediately challenged. But so is the text.

The sources for analysis are, this time, the opposite of scholarly readings. Rewritings of a story in children's Bibles, on the one hand, and in a popular commentary, on the other, show the interaction between what our culture teaches its younger members and how adult education reinforces this primary ideological insertion with the justifications of "reason." The issue that informs the textual problems, as will become clear shortly, is heroism. The hero Samson predetermines the structure of the story, and if that mechanism fails to work, the readers are in trouble. My hypothesis is, therefore, that there is an intimate relation between heroism as the expression and justification of patriarchy, and problems of representation of subjectivity. A shift in the concept of heroism from an instrumental view, in which the hero is sent by higher powers to represent their glory through pure physical acts, to a view wherein individualism and responsibility replace the lack of psychological concerns in the older view, puts the modern reader in a conflict that cannot be solved but by blaming the woman.

37

This shift implies yet another shift. The hero who is, in the instrumental view, the instrument of the higher father occupies a typical son-position. In the modern view, where the hero must justify, by his excellence, the excessive power he represents, his is rather a father position. He is often not yet a father figure, but one who shows that he deserves to become one. This change leads, in the readings we will study, to a blind defense of the hero as just such a modern hero, in other words, of his worthiness to be a paternal hero. This does not mean that he cannot be blamed; Samson is, for example, frequently blamed for stupidity—a leftover from his instrumental status as the blind executor of the father's commands. But the integrity of the hero as an ideal figure of power is to be saved at all costs—the efforts betraying, again, the problem they try to conceal. The tension between these two concepts of heroism, which the modern readers cannot entirely accommodate, leads to a negative interpretation of the hero's antagonist. The issues involved in the text when we accept its historical difference, however, do not require a positive versus a negative distribution of characters.

The problem of the hero, or the hero as problem, will be analyzed within the overall subjectivity of the text. Again, a careful analysis of the narrative structure, focusing on subject positions, allows us to interpret both the problematic textual features and the readings they yield. Differences between rewritings will, again, not be able to conceal a common concern, which, in one way or another, works against the woman.

Questions Asked and Problems Revealed

In our culture, the story of Samson and Delilah is the paradigmatic case of woman's wickedness. The combination of seduction, unfaithfulness, and treason is an unavoidable and fatal one. However strong a man is, and Samson *was* strong, he will always be helpless against woman's strategies of enchantment. Once seduced, he will be betrayed. This is how the myth of Samson and Delilah is naturalized. It is very easy to check this claim, since documents are numerous. From pop songs to children's Bibles, from ancient to modern commentaries, all through the history of literature, traces of the myth can be found that refer to these themes. I will not give a survey of what is already too obvious. I read a few Dutch children's Bibles, randomly chosen, one of which is a classic in Holland and written by the most popular author of children's books (W. G. van der Hulst, hereafter vdH). It dates from the beginning of this century, but it is still the most widely read book of its kind. The others are another classic (Anne de Vries, AdV) by an author of regional novels, one newer but still orthodox text (Evert Kuyt, EK), and two "modern" children's

Bibles (Y. L. Klink, YK, and Gertie Evenhuis and Nico Bouhuijs, EB) of the sort in which Jesus wears jeans and helps his mother wash the dishes. On the other hand, I took one commentary written for adults. The idea of this book (Naastepad 1970), which is entirely devoted to Judges 13–16, is to present a modern interpretation for general readers. It is not an exclusively theological discussion and is easily accessible; it has already had several reprints and is very well known.

The most striking feature common to these documents is the unanimity of their judgments. All the texts pronounce a moral judgment about the characters at the same diegetical moments. It is hardly surprising that those moments contain the events that "prove" the features retained in the myth. For example, Delilah is presented as beautiful at the moment when Samson's falling in love with her is mentioned but as false, unreliable, and greedy when the transaction with the Philistines is concluded. This observation, too, seems obvious. The mere fact that the view of the characters is presented in relation to their actions is a most common thing. What interests me here, however, is the reaction of the readers (the authors of the documents) to events on which the Bible itself makes no comment.

This response shows a to-and-fro movement in the process of mythification. Events that are not understandable without moral judgment, hence not naturalizable, are provided with a motivation by the readers; that very motivation in its turn naturalizes the moral judgment itself, thus enabling it to do its job and make the events not only understandable but utterly inevitable. Criticizing the myth, then, necessitates undoing the popular reading of those judgments and attempting to replace the seemingly self-evident motivations with others. This procedure is not meant, let me stress once more, to declare the better interpretation a "faithful" reading of the text. I am concerned not with what is *really written* but with why what is written is *thus read*.

In this view, the leading question derived from the narratological model is simply: *who does what?* In other words, which subject is the agent of which activity? This question provokes, within its answer, the following problems:

1. Speech: When agents speak, it is Delilah who has the initiative. Samson only reacts. This fact is in conflict with the common expectation that in a narrative the main character is the one who takes the initiative.
2. Perspective: When the agents are in conflict, the view of the events given is Delilah's. Samson's view of the main events is never represented.
3. Action: Application of the actantial model (Greimas 1965, 1970) poses

the problem of subject. If Delilah is considered as the subject, then there is not much left of Samson's "officially" recognized heroism, since then he does not act, does not strive, and does not accomplish. On the other hand, it is difficult to fill out the whole model if we consider Samson as the subject.

These problems can be transferred without difficulty to a nonscholarly level of reading. The questions raised are then:

1. Why does Samson not reproach Delilah for her betrayal?
2. Why does he accept Delilah's reproaches without giving his own view?
3. Why does he finally give her the crucial information, thus sealing his undoing, instead of acting to prevent it?

These three problems come together in a most crucial question raised by the catastrophe: why does he expect to be saved when he is shaved? Knowing that he has broken his contract with God, he still expects the other party to respect the contract and help him.

It is my claim that (1) all these whys have indeed been raised by the narratological questions about the subjects, and (2) they will lead to an analysis that allows me to account for the interaction between text and myth.

The analysis will be linear, following the text. Sometimes, however, anticipation and retrospection will be unavoidable. Indications for my interpretations are (1) the wording of the text, taken as literally as possible; (2) ambiguities in the strict sense, as defined by Rimmon (1977:3–76), and in the loose sense of double meanings, where both meanings will be considered; (3) narrative features that seem to conflict with the expectations of the genre (e.g., narrative). Theological as well as historical considerations are left aside.

In order to facilitate reading, a summary view of my interpretation now follows. Oppositions that cause tension are: the social versus the individual; relationship by blood versus relationship by law (marriage); masculine versus feminine. These oppositions are problematic because of a relation between sexuality and strength. The opposition between the social and the individual arises for the first time with the interpretation of Samson's riddle. The problem of relationship by blood versus relationship by law is involved in all three love affairs between Samson and women and in his relationship with his parents. The opposition between masculine and feminine is relevant for the analysis of Samson's character. The relation between strength and sexuality is obvious. It is the ground (in the common and the semiotic sense) of the events between Samson and Delilah. It is the form "love" takes in this story.

The Emergence of the Hero

In the beginning, Samson's mother is childless. Sterility was, in the period where the fabula is situated, a disaster for a woman. It deprived her of her status. One day, however, while her husband is absent, a messenger comes to tell her that she will be pregnant and give birth to a son. The messenger has the appearance of a man. He commands the woman to abstain from wine and unclean food, because the child will be a Nazirite, a man devoted to God. No razor is to touch his head. The commands will be in force "from the womb to the day of his death" (13:7).

The motif of late conception with God's help is quite frequent in the Bible. It contains two variants that occur separately or combined:

—the late conception of a previously sterile woman;
—the (asexual?) conception by God, in the absence of the husband.

The first happens, for example, to Rachel. She conceives only after giving up her sexual monopoly in favor of her sister Leah. Sarah conceives, extremely late, after the visit of a messenger, the moment she no longer feels any desire for her aging husband, as she explicitly says, "Shall I have pleasure, my lord being old also?" (Gen. 18:12). That is the second variant. And of course this event is repeated with Jesus' birth. In that example, the asexual nature of the conception is explicitly mentioned in Matt. 1:18 (see Warner 1976).

Naastepad (24) insists on the absence of the husband. He interprets it as a sign of an unsuccessful sexual relationship between husband and wife. The children's Bibles hardly mention this whole episode. Whether or not this omission may be considered as a form of censorship, the nonsexual conception seems a problem to all recipients. In the text, insistence on Manoah's absence, the command of purity, and the concordance with similar cases where nonsexuality is more overtly stressed, may be considered as symbolic expressions of a negativity. Purity, absence, and ellipses are all equally negative.

The First Woman

Samson falls in love with a Philistine woman. This creates some trouble at home. His parents would rather have him marry a woman of his own tribe. They resign themselves to his choice and the three of them go to Timnath, where the woman lives. Naastepad (35) reminds us that Timnath is the place where Judah (Gen. 38) deviated from his path to go whoring. The woman he visited turned out later to be his daughter-in-law. This observation gives evidence of the recipient's sensitivity to a

problem central to this episode: the intermingling of sexual and familial
relations. This topic will be elaborated below. While they are on their
way, Samson tears a threatening lion to pieces. "And he rent him as he
would have rent a kid" (14:6). His parents don't notice this act, and he
does not tell them. Not long after this, they come back for the marriage.
Samson goes "out of his way" (cp. Judah) to look at the carcass of the
lion and finds there is now honey in the body. He takes some of it and
eats it. He gives honey to his parents without saying where he found it.
Then there is a wedding.

A few details are striking here. Samson marries for "love," or, to be
more precise, for sexual attraction. He had only seen the woman, and
she pleased him immediately. He marries a Philistine woman, who lives
among "the uncircumcised." The marriage is against his parents' wish.
Marrying a foreigner, for sexual reasons, against his parents' will: he is
certainly emancipating himself. But we will have to return to the tearing
of the lion, analyzable into the motifs of Samson's strength, its sweet
reward, and secrecy. Naastepad's mentioning Judah at this point suggests that he is aware of an element of conflict here.

The wedding takes seven days. Thirty young men feast with Samson: a
bachelor party. Samson asks them a riddle: "Out of the eater came forth
meat and out of the strong came forth sweetness" (14:14). The stake
consists of clothes. The young men persuade the bride to entice "her
groom into telling her the answer." They threaten her. They feel misused as guests. The woman asks Samson, weeps, persists. Her argument:
love. If Samson really loved her, would he keep the answer a secret from
her while her fellow tribesmen are involved? (14–16). The recipients
of the text all insist on the element *love* in the argument, and they don't
mention the kinship argument at all. Probably they consider it as one and
the same argument—understandably, as we shall see. Samson defends
himself by alleging his secrecy toward his parents: "I have not told it to
my father nor my mother and shall I tell it thee?" (14:16). Finally he gives
in, the woman tells the answer to her fellow tribesmen, and the seventh
day they can reply to Samson: "What is sweeter than honey? and what is
stronger than a lion?" (14:18). But Samson is not fooled: "If ye had not
plowed with my heifer, ye had not found out my riddle."

A few motifs that occurred before come up again in these strange
events, in a more explicit manner. At the same time they mirror what will
happen again later. The motif of the *riddle,* its being kept a secret, and its
being divulged to male Philistines for the sake of love: all mirror the
secret between Samson and Delilah. The relation with the *parents* comes
up again in the very last sentence of the text. The meanings symbolized
by the *lion* and the *honey* crop up in other expressions and contribute
considerably to the overall meaning conveyed.

Asking riddles and finding the answers is a widely spread motif in myths and fairy tales. The case of the sphinx in *Oedipus Rex* is only one example in a tradition. Bettelheim (1976) relates riddles in fairy tales to sexual maturity: whoever knows the answer knows the mystery of woman and sexuality. In this view, the fact that Samson asks the riddle of bachelors, the night before his own wedding, could symbolize his claim to be, as a groom, better informed in sexual matters than his virginal companions. The young men don't know the answer: they are not mature yet. Their only resource is the woman. They threaten her into betraying her groom's secret.

The strategy used by the woman conforms to stereotypical female behavior. She whines. Here, all the recipients of the text are ready to blame. They agree that her love falls short: "Her fear was greater than her love" (AdV); "trying to flatter him, cheat him, being nasty to him" (AdV). "As soon as he had told her the answer, she stopped crying, smiled and went away" (YK). Naastepad, writing for adults, insists on the sexual side of the event: Samson has not yet possessed his bride, and it is doubtful whether he ever will. He is tricked by his desire. All documents mention the comparison, in Samson's reply to the woman, between parents and bride, but none of them specify its meaning. This proof of Samson's immaturity, in spite of his brave efforts to defy his parents, makes him unfit for marriage. But that meaning enters into conflict with the image of Samson as a hero, an image that Naastepad especially wishes to preserve at all costs—even the cost of contradiction. The woman manages to have her will, or rather the young men's will. Samson is explicit: they have plowed with his heifer. Plowing is a traditional symbol of sex; a heifer is an immature cow: a virgin. That heifer was Samson's property, a right that has been violated by the men. It begins to look very much like adultery. There is a verb in Dutch for "to commit adultery," which is literally "to go strange," to go with a stranger (*vreemd gaan*). That verb suggests an equivalence between Samson's behavior toward his parents and his bride's behavior toward him. The parents wanted him to stick to his own people; his bride teaches him a lesson by sticking to hers.

Thus a tension develops between *own* and *alien*. We can say that Samson's behavior shows a lack of semiotic competence. He is only aware of the simple opposition between two positive sides of the same *family relations*. He overlooks the fact that the negative sides count also. The complications called into being by this feature of meaning (according to Greimas 1970:141) create problems in the relations between all the parties involved. For Samson, the separation between kinship and affinity is not carried out clearly enough (Lévi-Strauss 1949). He involves his parents too much in his sexual relation: it is to them that he offers the honey. The sexual symbolism of honey is common, in the Bible (The

Song of Songs) and in other cultures (Lévi-Strauss 1966). On the other hand, Samson underestimates the same kinship attachments on his bride's side. Schematically, and with some freedom toward Greimas, this understanding can be summed up as follows: family relations are viewed in different ways by Samson and by the others who represent society (Table 2).

The complexity of this problem seems to be repressed by Naastepad, who simply skips the kinship problem in both the honey episode and the riddle, even though he gives an extensive analysis of almost every word of the text. His selection is sexually oriented, which is justified, but he leaves out the element that makes sex a problem, in order to be able to preserve Samson's sexual heroism.

Samson has understood this semiotic lesson—now that it is too late. He reacts in two ways. The Philistines shall have their price—the clothes (another maturity symbol)—for they have, after all, discovered the secret of sexuality. But the clothes will be acquired by means of the death of thirty other Philistines. The theft will be avenged by another theft, by

Table 2

For Samson:

OWN-------------------ALIEN

For society:

relation by marriage

(Samson) OWN --------------------- ALIEN (bride)

blood relations   blood relations

(parents) NOT ALIEN------------- NOT OWN (companions)

no relation

- - - - - - opposition
◄ — ► contradiction
———► implication
· · · · · · · · resulting relation

another violation of the right of property. Second, Samson leaves his bride. He returns home. The woman is now given to his best man. This outcome confirms the sexual interpretation: the companions kept more than clothes.

We are left with one other riddle: the riddle itself. As opposed to the riddle of the sphinx, this one is not logical, even after its answer is known. There are four features: there is no logical link between riddle and answer; the riddle refers to Samson's secret encounters with the lion; the answer has the form of a question; and the riddle is about strength and sweetness.

Sweetness is related to lust. Moreover, the honey is in the belly. Samson wants to take pleasure from the belly of the torn lion, without telling his parents. The tearing has positive consequences, a feature it shares with that other kind of tearing that gives pleasure: defloration. Samson was not willing to tell his bride the secret. This can be interpreted as follows. It is Samson who, in the riddle, relates pleasure to strength. But he wants that connection to be kept a secret from others. In spite of what he seems to think, the secret is, in fact, kept. For the answer, though correct, is extremely common and leaves out the most interesting detail. It only recounts a cliché: strong as a lion, sweet as honey. What is left out is exactly this: that Samson's strength leads to pleasure; that the strong lion must be torn before his (or her) belly delivers pleasure. This connection between physical strength and sexual pleasure, and the violence involved in both, which is Samson's real secret, must have sounded too familiar to the recipients of the text to be a problem worth mentioning. There was no explanation needed here, as the meanings were naturalized "naturally."

There is, however, a logic that relates the riddle to its answer at an unconscious level. It involves the relation between the individual or personal and the uncommon, and, on the other hand, that between the general and the commonplace. The meaning that the whole riddle-and-answer game represents for Samson, and for the recipients, is diagrammed in Table 3.

Table 3

This complex shows that for Samson there is a problem that impedes his socializing. He cannot make the transition from highly individual, personal experience to its intersubjective acknowledgment/recognition.

The interpretation of these details is based on yet another connection. Comparing the features of the lion with those of the bride, we see a striking resemblance (Table 4).

The number of common features makes it plausible to extend the resemblance to the last feature too. That makes the identity of the "strong one" problematic. Who is the strong one in the riddle, who in the answer? Not necessarily the same person. Intimidated by woman's mystery, Samson fears her as too strong. So strong, that he needs his enormous strength to acquire her honey.

The riddle-answer game and Samson's failing effort to keep his secret lead us to the conclusion that the riddle was too pretentious. In spite of his successful first attempt with the lion, Samson is not yet fully capable of tearing up his bride's hymen. For he offered his honey to his parents, thereby signifying that his sexuality was still too much oriented toward his parents. Instead of answering a riddle, as becomes a young man who is to be initiated into the secret of sexuality, he asks one.

One formal feature of the game raises a problem of interpretation for Naastepad. The riddle is in the form of a declarative sentence, while the answer is in the form of a question. This inversion of the usual forms is interpreted by this recipient as proof of the companions' immaturity: they can only ask questions, being not yet capable of answering. With respect to subject positions, this argument can only hold if it also applies to Samson, that is, if he too is still immature. This possibility contradicts his supposed superiority as a modern hero and is therefore repressed by the recipient. Considering the symbolic meaning of asking riddles, I assume that the form of the sentences should be taken as a sign in both cases. After Samson's overly ambitious question, he is corrected by the companions. Since they are the woman's relatives, the initiative is theirs. They show him how his semiotic knowledge is lacking, and why his victory over the lion is not yet sufficient, not definite enough.

What exactly has happened between the people at the wedding? The

Table   4

Feature	Lion	Bride (specification)
tearable	+	+ (hymen)
sweet in belly	+	+ (sex)
detached from parents	+	+ (alien tribe)
elsewhere	+	+ (Timnath)
strong	+	?

real Event behind these fictive events seems to be the destruction of Samson's strength by publicity. As soon as his strength is *known*, he is powerless. I will try to argue later on that what is symbolized here is a form of the so-called *double standard*, according to which man has sexual freedom while woman has to stay strictly monogamous. In this morality, then, fear of knowledge about man's sexual performance could very well lead to the fear of its becoming banal, a fear that would make man feel so insecure that it would destroy his "strength." What can be done must not be spoken about, not be focalized. I will return to this point.

Samson gives up his bride and returns to the parental home. After some time he wants to go and pay her a visit. Then he wants to sleep with her. Her father will not allow it, for in the meantime she has been given to Samson's best man. Samson reacts; his response is translated in the New English Bible as, "Now shall I be more blameless than the Philistines, though I do them a displeasure," or in the RSV: "This time I will settle my score with the Philistines; I will do them some real harm" (15:3). In the Hebrew text the idea of Samson being within his rights "this time" is more explicit. He sets the Philistine crops on fire, an act that is answered by the Philistines' burning to death of the woman and her father (for an extensive interpretation of this revenge, see Bal Ms.).

This sequel seems to imply that Samson is still not ready for marriage. The companions, who did not create any problems about sex and managed to get the required information the right way, i.e., via the woman instead of via personal strength or big talk (the riddle), are the ones who have acquired the woman. Samson was mistaken in his reckoning. This man who had such difficulty in favoring legal ties above blood relationships is paid back in kind: his bride, too, prefers blood relations to relations by marriage. The access to sexuality is denied him by the male relatives of the desired woman. On the other hand, Samson has already gone too far in his efforts toward emancipation to be able to accept this second loss. He takes revenge.

The strange detail here, ignored by all recipients, is his insistence on his right of revenge "this time." We remember his first revenge. He killed thirty Philistines because the companions had plowed with his heifer. The insistence on "this time" suggests a return of the repressed feelings of guilt about the previous time, when, he now feels, he was not so clearly in the right. That guilt feeling supports the interpretation of the riddle as boasting. It suggests that the companions were right to answer the riddle via the bride. We should also remember that Samson was then the one who left the woman behind, feeling he was as yet inadequate. If he returns to her now, he feels ready for the relationship, *this time*. But the Philistines are not convinced. The father offers his younger daughter to him instead, relegating him to a younger age-group, thus symbolically signifying to him that he still has to grow up a little.

This time his revenge is justified indirectly. He takes it quite seriously: he indirectly kills the woman and the father-in-law who had rejected him. Samson was convinced of his maturity before the other was; that is why he cannot accept the rejection. This tension between his own (conscious) conviction and the understanding of it by the other will be an issue too in the Delilah episode. This time, Samson definitively gives up the marriage. The woman loses her life in the process, which is a considerable price to pay, but for Samson the more important loss is the cutting off, definitively, of the possibility of a satisfactory conclusion to this first sexual adventure. Needless to say, the discrepancy between the punishment that befalls the woman and Samson's own retreat points to the said double standard, which we have already seen at work and which we shall meet again. Naastepad comments (48, 49): "The woman has failed to leave her parents," and "Samson *burns* for love and so he can only *burn* the Philistine grounds." The recipient has no problem in accepting the revenge; on the contrary, he approves of it. The children's Bibles mention the whole episode in one sentence, with the exception of Klink's, which suppresses it completely.

The hostility between the two tribes is now complete. I will not go into details about the struggle between the circumcised Jews and the uncircumcised Philistines, presented in 15:7–20. For our argument the most important idea is the fact that the struggle has been caused by Samson's unsuccessful attempt at emancipation, and that, as specified in 14:4, the sequence of events is what God, presented thus as the episode's *destinateur,* had wished to happen. The father stipulates the limits of the hero's competence.

The Second Woman

The second relationship between Samson and a woman is represented very briefly. The limited interest of this woman is symbolized by her anonymity. The first woman was his (legal) wife, this one is a prostitute. Thus the two opposites in the scale of values that a woman can derive from her relations to a man are represented. The sequel is interesting in light of Freud's remarks on the need of many men for debasement in love. If respectable women make men impotent, the prostitute, because she claims no respect, can cure the problem. I will not insist on the social implications of this separation between affection/respect and sex, which is obvious but nonetheless disastrous. Freud defensively calls the separation "universal" (*allgemein*), thus mythifying a variable ideologeme. The idea seems to appeal to Naastepad. He celebrates the prostitute's continuous sexual availability and finds her therefore an example to the Philistine bride, who "refused Samson." Van der Hulst does not describe the woman but only her house, which he calls "a dangerous place"; de Vries indicates her as "a woman Samson knew," and Kuyt as "a bad woman." The two women have not only anonymity in common but also adultery. The bride committed it symbolically, by betraying the secret of Samson's alleged strength. The prostitute is defined by it. The bride did it for safety, but indirectly for money: the companions' money. The prostitute is defined as doing it for money. The bride was committed to her blood relations; the prostitute is defined by a complete lack of commitment, and a lack of relations.

The identity of the traitor is not mentioned. It is plausible to assume that it is the prostitute. Samson is in her house; she knows the secret. This leads to yet another point the women have in common. In both cases, Samson is in the house of the other. Samson does not bring his women into his own house, but he settles in theirs. This move points to a further effort of emancipation from his family, but at the same time it makes him vulnerable.

The betrayal, the danger, the ambush all take place during the night of love. Two reasons can be alleged for the anonymity of the traitor. The more superficial one is the prostitute's base position. As a person who is not respectable, she would then be denied the important narrative positions of actantial subject and narrator. A second reason could be the self-evident nature of the culprit's identity: the woman. Symbolically, however, the traitor could be Samson himself. He betrays himself by choosing once again a foreign woman; he again dares to try to have sex without his parents' consent. Whoever actually betrays him, the fact is that love makes Samson vulnerable, weak.

This time, too, the *knowledge,* the publication of Samson's sexual activities, seems to destroy his strength. Again, the only way to recover it is to leave the woman prematurely. This recovery of his strength is symbolized by the tearing up of the city gates. Thereby, at least symbolically, the woman is broken open. As a consequence the city-woman is not dangerous anymore. The symbolic equivalence of woman and city needs no substantiation since the writings of Freud; in the Bible, the symbol is extensively present. Jerusalem is often called a woman, often a prostitute. Samson carried the city gates to the holy city of Hebron. In order to be able to guarantee his safety with women, however, he had to break off prematurely. So he still does not know the answer to the companions' question: "What is sweeter than honey? and what is stronger than a lion?"

Samson and Delilah

Samson falls in love for the third time. This third woman does not have a specified social status. She is neither the respectable wife nor the despicable prostitute. But she has a name. Contrary to tradition, she is not presented as somebody's daughter. She is just Delilah, a woman that Samson loves. This suggests that Samson is at least capable of loving a woman for herself. According to most commentaries, she is also a Philistine, therefore a foreigner. She possesses her own house, and she is in contact with the Philistine chiefs. So, though she is not defined in relation to men, she seems to be well-to-do.

The relation between Samson and Delilah is not commented upon. Samson falls in love with her. More details are not called for. Samson now seems mature enough for love, for the definite separation from his parents. The ellipsis, the striking silence about the nature of the relationship, represents its own evidence. But Samson is a God-devoted Nazirite, and that pact is not so easily dealt with.

The Philistines take action as soon as they find out that Samson is in the city. They offer Delilah money. She accepts their bargain and begins her efforts to find the secret of Samson's strength. Now Delilah has things in common with the two previous women. She shares with the bride her willingness to make a deal with her fellow tribesmen, who want to destroy Samson. With the second woman, the prostitute, she has a motive in common: money. In fact, there is a riddle again: the riddle of Samson's strength, symbolically signified the first time, explicitly stated this time. The difference is in the actantial subject: the first time Samson took the initiative with the riddle, but this time his enemies do so. Having an idea about where to look, they try again via the woman.

Delilah's acceptance of the deal is *the* shocking detail in this episode. It gives evidence of Delilah's wickedness, and consequently of women's unreliability. The documents are most explicit. In the children's Bibles, Delilah is presented straightaway as a bad woman. She is beautiful (how would the hero otherwise fall in love with her?) but incapable of love (EB). She is false (VdH), a cheat (VdH), a hypocrite pretending love (AdV). Her likeness to the prostitute is underlined; she has many lovers (EB), is engaged to many men (EB), and is greedy (VdH, AdV); she is a slut (EB). Naastepad insists on Delilah's desirability, her beauty, and starts off by defending Samson's stupidity in falling into her trap: she is just irresistible (64) and behaves accordingly. She provokes him with coquetry, pretending to refuse him and thus exciting him more (64). Needless to say, the text does not give the slightest hint that would support these assumptions. No judgment is pronounced; the "ellipsis," the gap, the simple mention of Samson's falling in love without any particular reason, makes naturalization impossible. This is how gap-reading works. Additions have to be made, and they have to denigrate Delilah in order to justify Samson as a "proper," that is, paternal, hero. The actantial initiative, his power as a subject, is thus taken from him in the same move.

The resemblance between Delilah and the prostitute, however, is merely superficial in the text. It is just obvious enough to set the said naturalization in motion. On closer inspection, there is even an opposition. A prostitute receives money for her love, and the love has to be without commitment. Delilah, on the other hand, was already committed when she was asked to give up love for money. A second difference concerns social status. We have seen that, named by a name of her own and in possession of a house, associating with high-placed people, she could be considered a prototype of the socially successful, independent woman. Her bargain with the chieftains then looks more like a business transaction than a low betrayal. In wartime, and it is such a time, no blame is attached to patriotism. Delilah just uses her specific potential for helping her tribe and makes enough money out of it to preserve her financial independence. Only Klink gives patriotism as a possible motive. Naastepad is obviously in trouble here. He has to blame Delilah in order to defend Samson, but at the same time she has to be worth the hero's love. How does he deal with the idea of bribery?

Concentrating his commentary on the love theme, this recipient simply ignores the relation between Delilah and the chieftains. He warns against a moralistic response, which seems peculiar. The reason is that he interprets the whole episode as a lesson about love, presenting Samson as an expert (strength is for Naastepad as well as for the hero a proof of good lovemaking) and Delilah as a perfect, because desirable, woman. Several times this interpretation forces oblique reasoning on him. In order to deal with the bribery, for example, he argues: "The text of this chapter does not especially aim at teaching us how deceitful the sly seductions of woman can be. *For that we know already by other sources, if direct experience has not taught it to us yet*" (64; italics mine). This way, the recipient enables himself both to preserve the stress on sex and the hero's heroism, and to naturalize Delilah's guilt even more strongly than the others do. For not only is it that woman in general is held responsible for what happens, but her wickedness is presented as self-evident, and so beyond discussion, even beyond particularization, and therefore apparently trivial. Wicked-by-nature woman is thus denied participation in the narrative events. Such is the logic that integrates two incompatible views of heroism between which Delilah is caught.

The First Attempt

Delilah asks Samson where his strength is located. Her question is surprisingly outspoken. She wants to know how he can be mastered. The Hebrew verb used for "master" is, significantly, the verb that is also used in the sense of "to rape" (e.g., the rape of Tamar by Amnon in 2 Sam.

13). Samson's reply is: "If they bind me. . . ." The third-person pronoun indicates clearly that Samson has understood the goal of Delilah's question. He knows perfectly well that she is talking not about some love game but about his being mastered by the other, the enemy. None of the recipients account for this frankness, and the consequences it implies as to Samson's responsibility.

Samson replies with a lie. In this lie, however, he uncovers more of himself than we might think. He says: "If they bind me with seven fresh bowstrings not yet dry, then I shall become as weak as any other man" (16:7). He still conceals in this answer the exact location of his strength, but he does reveal its nature. The strength is his exceptionality. That strength will be destroyed as soon as the other finds out how relative and restricted it is. This situation reminds us of the riddle at Samson's wedding. It also reminds us of the tree in paradise, the forbidden tree of knowledge of good and evil. There, too, there is a connection between the man and woman relationship, knowledge and guilt (woman's guilt, according to the generally naturalized interpretation). Is there such a connection between man and woman, and good and evil, in the present case too?

Meanwhile, let us examine Samson's lie further. He talks of fresh bowstrings. Bowstrings are binders made out of organic material. Their structure is simple, in contrast to the binders he will mention the second time. Samson insists that the strings must be fresh. For the moment we retain these details, which receive their specific meaning only when compared to the other answers. Delilah now binds Samson with fresh bowstrings. There are Philistines in her room. Clearly, Delilah cannot bind Samson unless he is asleep. That reminds us of the Gaza episode and its meaning: love makes one weak. Delilah wakes Samson up with the words, which are to be taken literally, "The Philistines are upon you, Samson," words that she will repeat three more times. Here again, Delilah makes not the slightest attempt to conceal her betrayal. Samson is lucky that he had lied to her. He can unloose himself easily. We could even say: he had not completely surrendered to love, so that he can still unbind the engagement. At least this is the reproach that Delilah will use later.

The Second Attempt

In 16:10 Delilah indeed blames Samson. "You have been laughing at me and telling me lies." The main reproach is that he has not taken her seriously, and Delilah feels hurt. Hearing such a reproach would suggest that Samson has at least been unfaithful to her or disdained her love. The only crime he is guilty of is that of trying to save his own life by responding to betrayal by lying. He does not, however, maintain this in his defense.

This silence leads us to one of the reading problems derived from the narratological problems. Why does Samson refrain from defending himself against such unjust reproaches? Why does he not attack Delilah in turn, just as subsequent readers do? In narratological terms: why does he not take the initiative of speech? Why does the text not present his view of the events, since he is the hero? Significantly, none of the recipients notice a problem here. For the moment, there is but one plausible explanation: that is, silence signifies consent. Samson says nothing because he has nothing to say, no reproach. His point of view is not given because it has been given, in Delilah's.

Samson's reply to Delilah's renewed question about the source of his strength is almost a repetition of his first reply. Again a new, unused binder is needed, this time in the form of ropes. Again he stresses that, when the appropriate binder is used, he will be weak "like any other man." Delilah believes him. That means that she must be sensitive to the difference between the two binders. If we take the detail of the different ropes to be significant, they must have meaning, not only as binders, but in their difference—here, the difference between simple and complex. The intertwined rope suggests a bond between its constituents that is not easy to unbind. These details may be read on a symbolic level. The new, the unused is related to virginity. It is hardly likely that this independent and desirable woman is a virgin. Who is, then? Indeed, Samson has paid a visit to the prostitute in Gaza—a visit that was, however, prematurely interrupted—and he is already involved with Delilah, but somehow, according to the logic of metonymy, he must be virginal. How? Guided by the principle of detail and difference, we must try to discover the answer: through the binders' symbolic meaning.

Binders allow bonds. Samson's virginity could then be related to his inability to become emotionally involved. This interpretation is supported by further events. The bowstrings were insufficient because of their simple structure. The rope symbolizes, both in its function as a binder and its structure as such, the intertwining of a love that is not based only on uncommitted sex, a symbol that we know from different cultures (see, for example, the Indian snake *metuna*, the snake-god lovers with intertwined tails). The shift from bowstrings to rope indicates a progress in Samson's emotional development. That is why Delilah believes him.

The following events are identical to the previous ones.

The Third Attempt

Third time lucky is not only a common cliché but a deeply rooted symbolism also found in the Bible. An instance is presented in 2 Sam. 9 and 2 Sam. 14:5–11. The number three has different symbolic meanings, two of which may be interesting here. Bettelheim (1976) explains it as the position of the child in the nuclear family. A less specific but related meaning is completeness in general. According to this symbolism, the third attempt should succeed. This is not the case. Or is it?

Delilah casts the same reproaches on Samson as she did on the previous occasion. Again Samson offers nothing in his defense and does nothing to blame Delilah. And again he lies. This time his answer is: "If thou weavest the seven locks of my head with the web" (16:13). This answer is still a lie, but less and less so. The first striking detail is the use of the second-person pronoun, making the discursive situation a personal one (Benveniste 1966, Tamir 1976). Both lovers are aware that the issue of the struggle is Samson's betrayal to the Philistines. The shift from impersonal to personal language points to an awareness, on another level of consciousness, that the relationship with Delilah is the "real issue" at stake. Will she be able to bind him, and so help him to overcome his reserved attitude toward a complete relationship? Let us take a look at the binder.

The binders show a progression not only in their capacity for binding but also in the complexity of their symbolic force. *Seven* is the number of fullness, in a variety of cultures. Locks (the Hebrew specifies that the locks are tressed) consist of hair. Weaving is a stronger—because more complex—way of holding things together than binding. The weaving loom is traditionally a metonymical symbol of women. It points to domestic labor, family life, and spatial confinement.

This symbol can be analyzed into a psychoanalytical and social meaning. In other words: psychoanalytic meanings have social implications. In yet other words: socially speaking, the loom represents private life as opposed to social life. Psychoanalysis allows us to think of the long hair of women. There are fairy tales in which women weave their own hair. Integrating both meanings, we might suggest the following interpretation. Traditionally, woman is the master indoors, man, in society. In such a view it becomes understandable that man is afraid of being bound too long or too firmly to private life. For many men, work, rather than family life, is a safe harbor. Fear of emotional attachment because it means imprisonment can make such a man reserved. Hair is often considered a constitutive feature of woman's sex appeal. Baudelaire and Mallarmé, both in their own symbolic networks, demonstrate the ambivalence of this appeal, and Freud explains it. The warp of the web comes, then, close to Delilah's hair. The weaving represents the interlacement of the hair of both lovers during sleep.

All these details may be read today within a psychoanalytic framework. More and more Samson is expressing his own fears. Is hair the attraction of woman, so much so that it can entangle you? Freud implied this idea in comparing their hair, via pubic hair, to the vagina as a representation of the dangers of too committed a love: the *vagina dentata,* that phantas-magoric horror for men who fear to lose the penis and, synecdochically, the self. The psychoanalytical meaning has as its social side the idea of the trap of the permanent relationship that imprisons the victim. The traditional symbolism city-house-room-vagina receives in this tale an ab-solutely renewed, concrete force.

We are not finished with the hair motif. Delilah's hair has been brought to the fore, in the loom, as a symbol of her dangerous attraction. But the tale is about Samson's hair. The reader who knows the tale is already aware that his hair is the source of his strength, a strength that seems to be connected with masculinity. Samson and Delilah resemble each other: her feminine and dangerous attraction, his masculine and dangerous strength, are both located in the hair. According to Freud, the cutting of hair is a symbol of castration, and, to see the socially active implications of this psychoanalytic symbolism, we can look at some middle-aged gentle-men who have been plunged into midlife crises by the fear that they will not be taken seriously anymore in sexual matters because of their reced-ing hairlines. An unexpected link between castration anxiety and the "hair envy" that opposes older to younger men is suggested by this phenomenon. We might even conjecture that the shift from one form of heroism to another fits into this competition between generations of men (for a detailed discussion, see Bal Ms.). The Nazirite vow relates the growing of hair to abstinence. In that vow, the fear of castration receives symbolic expression.

The forbidden razor comes very close now. So close, that we can safely say that Samson has indeed betrayed his secret already. He senses it himself, for he does not finish his sentence. The readers react to this "castrated" sentence in various ways: none is indifferent to it. The trans-lators of the Jerusalem Bible edition have neglected this sign (or re-pressed it), for they finish the sentence that is incomplete in Hebrew. So do the children's Bibles. Naastepad, on the other hand, carefully trans-lating from the Hebrew, notices the incompleteness of the sentence and significantly explains it as a sign of Delilah's impatience. That interpreta-tion shows that this recipient is sensitive to the likeness between the two protagonists, since he can even interchange them. Samson is speaking, not Delilah. Her supposed impatience is not explained any further, but the author is aware of the confessional nature of the lock-symbol, since he finishes: "The crucial element is now introduced. Death is imminent" (69). So, third time lucky? Samson's surrender to women is symbolized as inevitable, experienced as it is as imprisonment in the *vagina dentata,* private life, love. That love is symbolized this way signifies that Samson's attitude toward it is still ambivalent. He surrenders, but reluctantly. For Samson the tearer is himself torn.

If this interpretation is correct, as far as Samson goes, the most important thing has been said and, with the help of the magic of language, *done*. Then why is the fourth attempt needed?

The Fourth Attempt

Returning to the initial questions, we may ask again: why does Samson give the crucial information, aware as he must be of the use Delilah will make of it? This reading problem is related to the narratological question of the actantial subject: who is, in this episode, the subject, who the *destinateur*? If we attribute the actantial subjectivity to Delilah, her object is the acquisition of the desired information. Attribution of the *destinateur* function is then not self-evident. A theoretical problem inherent in this actant is the difference in interpretation it allows. Between the incentive at the beginning of the fabula and the arbiter at the end, there is an enormous difference. Delilah's incentive is the Philistine proposition; the arbiter is Samson himself. For he is the only one who knows the secret, and on him depends Delilah's success. This problem sheds a different light on Delilah's narrative program. She remains the subject of this episode, but as such she is, in the fabula as a whole, only the executor of a struggle between two male forces. Her function is to bring those two together.

This interpretation is not wholly satisfactory. The Philistines are men, but, referred to as the uncircumcised, they represent impurity. As blood relations of all Samson's sexual partners, they represent pleasure as well, the pleasure that was until now represented by women only. This link between women and the uncircumcised will turn out to have a specific meaning. The likeness is stressed in the name: "Philistine" connotes "undifferentiated."

Meanwhile, Delilah feels deceived. She does not only reproach Samson for not taking her seriously. She blames him for not *loving* her. "How canst thou say, I love thee, when thine heart is not with me?" We recognize this reproach. Samson's bride harassed him with the same one. It is not absolutely new in this case either, if we realize with Lacan that "toute demande est demande d'amour." Love, in this view, has two features: it is full, whole, absolute, and it is surrender.

For several days Delilah harasses Samson with her demand for full surrender. Samson says nothing. His heart shrinks, "his soul was shortened unto death" (16:16). This very pointed expression is to be taken in all its strength. Samson is in mortal danger. What exactly is the danger? Delilah's demand, her conception of love, scares him. Psychoanalytically, the demand for total surrender inspires the fear of being completely absorbed, swallowed. That fear has already been symbolized in the loom.

Rank (1924) explains that fear by the birth trauma. This explanation allows us to account for the ambivalence of the fear too. For the phantasma of the return to the womb is also attractive. The fear, then, is applied to the inevitable new separation that is to follow the return. Escape from the woman's vagina, room, house, city is also a way of keeping ahead of fate.

Socially, Delilah's conception of love is traditionally feminine. It is woman who is supposed to surrender to man. Samson knows very well that the surrender demanded is surrender to the Philistines. This attracts attention to the unclear differentiation of sexes: the Philistines are men. So much ambivalence offers Samson an as yet psychologically impossible alternative. As we have seen, it was very difficult for him to actualize his heterosexuality. He thought he had reached maturity with Delilah. Now new ambivalent tendencies, new drives, new aspects come to the fore. Samson has to surrender if he wants to love, but to whom or to what?

Samson has already revealed his secret. Still, Delilah's criticism makes him very unhappy. When Samson was, sometime after his unsuccessful wedding, convinced of having reached sexual maturity, he did not manage to convince the Other, represented by the bride's father. The same thing happens here. Samson is so unhappy because he is confronted with a split in his self. What he knows but comfortably keeps unconscious, thanks to the fact that "the story is a revelation and a concealment at once" (Mooij 1975:93), is simply not explicit enough for the other. Samson's problem is the problem of language. There is an unbridgeable gap between the ego and the other. That gap is symbolized in numbers. He has spoken three times, and thus attained completeness. For Delilah, who represents the Other, a fourth time is needed. A fourth time, in which language cannot operate indirectly, but in which unconscious conflicts have to be brought into the open, however destructive they may be. Three times for Samson, four times for the other. The trinity of the nuclear family is sacrificed to the alienating relationship with the other, the fourth person. Only then can man attain maturity. The myth of Samson symbolizes the entry into the symbolic order.

Samson's definite answer displays a few significant motifs. I quote the passage in full: "There hath not come a rasor upon mine head; for I have been a Nazirite unto God from my mother's womb: if I be shaven, then my strength will go from me, and I shall become weak, and be like any other man" (16:17).

The surrender of "all his heart" (16:18) starts with the mention of the razor. That instrument of castration is the fatal weapon. What is needed is not an increasingly stronger tie but the opposite: absolute separation. The mention of the Nazirite vow points to the vow of purity of this God-devoted man. The vow holds "from my mother's womb." Samson himself relates these details to the already mentioned relative nature of his strength. Without his seven (phallic) locks he is weak, like any other man. Consequently, *with* these locks he has a very special relationship with God, based on purity. But this relationship is crossed with another one: with this lock he is bound to woman too. Without the lock, there remains very little of his masculine force. What have these two motifs to do with one another?

First, there is the question of Delilah's belief. Three times she has been cheated, and she knows the definite character of the number three as in a symbol. Still the text tells us: "And when Delilah saw that he had told her all his heart" (16:18). The verb *to see* is important, since it thematizes focalization. Delilah has insight into the nature of Samson's love. She has seen something that she had not seen the third time. The third time Samson had, however, mentioned all the crucial elements: the link with hair, fear of bonds, fear of woman. One element was still lacking, which is now mentioned. That is the mother's womb. This new element shows her the link between haircutting, powerlessness, and becoming like any other man. For Samson, she sees, it is not an even tighter bond with a woman that helps him out of his problem, but the separating of a bond, the precise nature of which is not yet quite clear, but which has to do with the mother's womb, castration, and the Nazirite vow.

Samson's Death

Samson knows from experience that Delilah is betraying him. Nevertheless, he falls quietly asleep, "on her knees," an expression in Hebrew that also allows the translation "between her knees." This attitude on Delilah's lap shows that he has completely surrendered to her indeed. The attitude suggests in the first place rest after lovemaking. The attitude is also that of a *pietà*. In his painting of the scene, Rubens stresses the sexual side by attributing to Samson's face a thoroughly satisfied expression, and, on the other hand, by adding an *entremetteuse*. Rembrandt goes even further. He also adds the matchmaker and depicts a man, a Philistine, who is cutting Samson's hair. The naked breasts and the attitudes of Delilah and the Philistine suggest intimacy between them. In Rembrandt's painting, both sex and motherhood are strongly suggested. As we have seen before, love makes one powerless, very literally so. Full surrender sets the castrating razor in motion. Delilah does not handle it herself. She holds Samson in an embrace. The indiscreet penetration of other men in the room of love is now a fact.

Again, the castrator is embodied in knowledge of the secret. This castration-by-intersubjectivity is now directly personified by the Philistine in the room. Looking back at the wedding, we notice the same motifs, represented more explicitly this time. The woman betrays Samson's secret to her male blood relations, and thus saps his special strength. By cutting off his locks, the temporary weakness of the penis is made permanent.

Samson's attitude on/between Delilah's knees with his hair next to her pubic hair has still another meaning. When Samson is awakened by Delilah with the words, "The Philistines be upon thee, Samson," he says that again God will help him escape as in the previous times. This confidence, this absolute absence of guilt, is surprising. Samson knows very well that this time he has betrayed his secret. He can be sure that when he wakes up, he will find himself shaved, just as he was bound and woven earlier. Nevertheless, he has gone to sleep with Delilah, and he now still expresses his confidence in God. The solution the recipients choose is his lack of intelligence. There is not the slightest indication in the text that Samson is stupid, but this naturalization is understandable in cultures where ideology prescribes an opposition between nature and culture, that is, strength and intelligence for men, beauty and intelligence for women. As in the case of the absence of Samson's view, I prefer to take the text's subjectivity seriously first. If Samson does not feel guilty, if he does not take into consideration that on his side the pact has been broken, then that is, within the fabula, the truth. Then he cannot be guilty, and he *is* entitled to God's help. How is this possible?

The expression "on/between the knees" (of a woman) is used at other places in the Bible. In Gen. 30:3, Rachel, who, like Samson's mother, was initially sterile, says to her husband Jacob: "Behold my maid Bilhah, go in unto her; and she shall bear upon my knees, that I may also have children by her."

This quotation shows two things. The expression is related to childbirth. Women gave birth on their knees; midwives are said to hold women on their knees. Second, it proves that the expression is used symbolically. If the maid will give birth, that delivery will be symbolically Rachel's and it will enforce her position. Use of the expression in the crucial scene of the Samson tale gives the key to the interpretation of Samson's strange confidence in God. He *is* innocent. We now remember the words he uttered when betraying his secret: "from my mother's womb." This too has to be taken textually. *From* means *after* birth, not before, not during. Picturing the character Samson at the moment of the haircutting, we notice that he displays a strange likeness to a baby: he is bald, weak, sleeping, speechless, and he is resting on/between the knees of the one woman in the story who is defined in relation to him, not to others. He wakes up *after* the haircutting. It is also possible to say: he is born after the haircutting. This interpretation is acceptable in the framework of the psychoanalytic theory of the birth trauma and the fantasy of rebirth.

Reacting to Freud's remarks on the subject, Rank devoted a book to the birth trauma as early as 1924. The first feature of birth is radical separation. This concept is related to the solution of Samson's secret: no bond is strong enough, separation is needed. The traumatic experience of this fundamental event can lead to different consequences, in which fear, desire, and repression are combined. Fear of being swallowed again, which would necessitate a renewal of the traumatic separation. Desire to be adopted again into the safe and warm womb. Fear of being stuck there. These fears and this desire are often intermingled inextricably. Fear signifies desire as desire signifies fear. Repression easily leads to repression of the role of woman in the event, to minimalizing it, or to trying to take away in other fields the power she apparently has over human reproduction. Rank states it explicitly: repression of the birth trauma leads to oppression of women.

One fantasy often met with is the childish idea that the mother has first eaten the child, since the thought that he has always been in the womb is unbearable. That fantasy allows the child to indulge in fear and aggression. But above all, it leaves the possibility that man too can give birth, for he too can eat and excrete. In any case, Rank's study shows the interest men have in talking women into the idea of penis envy: their own feeling of uterus envy, deeper and more difficult to avoid, can be effectively repressed with the help of a projected penis envy.

For the crucial scene in the Samson story, the following elements of this theory are important. The birth trauma leads to contradictory feelings. Fear of repetition and desire for return compete. Fear may enhance the fantasy of the *vagina dentata,* socially expressed in the fear of lasting relationships and emotional involvement. Desire may lead to the desire for sexual penetration, which is, in part, a return. Therefore a woman is also mother to a man. Both Rubens's and Rembrandt's paintings have this connotation. But since the return can never be perfect, the pleasure is never perfect either, and the feelings include ambivalence.

An explanation of Samson's inner peace, his confidence in God, and his acceptance of Delilah's betrayal is now available. Delilah has not betrayed him. She has helped him to be reborn. The bond with God was a symbiotic one: God is part of the self. This close bond between Samson and his own self is what he wanted to escape from. This is why he tried to live with women. Woman represents in this case the Other who gives access to the symbolic order. Lacan (1966:445) stresses the social, the intersubjective, and the preexistent and hence impersonal aspects of the symbolic order. "C'est à l'énormité de cet ordre à quoi nous sommes, si l'on peut dire, nés une seconde fois . . . : soit l'ordre symbolique constitué par le langage, et le moment du discours universel concret" (It is the enormity of this order that we are, so to speak, born a second time . . . : the symbolic order constituted by language and the moment of universal concrete discourse). The paradox in Lacan's two orders is that the one that is not impersonal (the imaginary order of the symbiosis with the mother) is also the prepersonal one: the subject has not yet been formed. There is no space left, then, for the strictly personal; we fall from one dependency into the next.

This relativization of the romantic myth of individuality helps to insert Samson's mythical but secret strength into a wider problem. The symbolic order is intersubjective; it enables one, but also forces one, to go outside oneself. Lacan speaks of a *birth* into the symbolic order, a rebirth. We have already noticed that Delilah's being-other, being the Other, forced Samson to round out the pseudo-completeness of the nuclear family with a fourth position, a shift that entailed his making the unconscious conscious. The third time, his expression was self-expression, not an intersubjective story: it was still too exclusively indexical and hence too strongly "bound" to himself as a unique subject. The rebirth in Delilah's lap is not only a return to the mother's womb. It is a return that cuts off wrong choices and enables him to begin anew. *Reculer pour mieux sauter.* However, it is still a return, a regression. The paradox, or the third riddle, of this text is the result of this move. Samson's rebirth leads to imprisonment and powerlessness, shortsightedness, symbolized in his blinding and womanlessness. What goal has he then reached?

To find that out, a return to Samson's sexual problems is required. The site of his sexual power was its secret. Knowledge destroyed it. The revelation makes him impotent, powerless, *banal.* The banal is unacceptable for this proud man. In that, he is like those men who try to compensate for their violent envy of childbirth by social and sexual boasting. But if the commonplace is unacceptable, social life is impossible. Intersubjectivity is only possible thanks to *shared* knowledge. A solution to this seemingly impossible dilemma could be the absolute possession of the social order. As long as woman is excluded from the community, it is not really *common.*

This principle explains the double standard. Man's sexual performance is common, relative, and that is disturbing. This fact has to be kept a secret. Monogamy for women is the only way to achieve this objective. The same holds for social life. Man's performances in public life do not have to be extraordinary, so long as his wife overestimates them. The more she is confined to the house, the greater the chance of success.

One performance is inaccessible to men. Childbirth. *The* phantasma, the ideal hidden behind so much ambition, is man giving birth to a child. That event is, however, possible on a symbolic level. For a man like Samson, who constantly has to balance his relationships with women against his pact with himself/God, rebirth is not yet enough. What he seeks is to identify, while giving birth himself, with the child being born: autogenesis. What he would perform then is the impossible but highly desirable ideal of making a harmonious whole out of the conflicts of life. To stay in himself *and* go out; to bring the symbolic order into the imaginary order; to make a symbiosis out of a separation. Clearly, the rebirth on Delilah's lap is not a fulfillment of this ideal. It is only a preparatory phase.

What exactly is the fate Samson accepts with such peace of mind? He is blinded, imprisoned, forced to labor. He is made to walk in circles all day long. Turning around, confined, blinded, his life now seems cut off from women. His features are now, however, not so much those of a newborn babe as those of a not-yet-born fetus. The woman is not excluded but including, albeit symbolically.

The last scene, Samson's death, gives a solution to the remaining problems. His hair has grown again. No Philistine has thought to keep him bald. In this interpretation it is not necessary to explain this omission with the sledgehammer argument of Philistine stupidity, as Naastepad does. They simply cannot reach him, since he is not yet born. And they do not find it necessary, since Samson's hair is no longer related to heterosexuality. Meanwhile, his strength comes back, but it is a different strength. Until now, Samson used to go *elsewhere* for sex. He went to live in the house of the woman. But since he was not yet finished with his origins, his parents, the transition failed. Now he is inside, at home, in his own private atmosphere, autistically turning around. The strength he is now saving up will not be used with a woman ("out of the eater came forth meat") but against her.

Samson's last, third, real and symbolically ideal birth is his death. For what happens? He is standing between two pillars. From the perspective of a newborn child, the mother's thighs, several times larger than the baby's head, must be enormous. During birth, the opening between the thighs is small, too small, oppressively tight. Samson corrects the act of birth: he forces open a larger gap. In the process, the pillar-thighs break. This is, as the text explicitly states, Samson's greatest *tour de force*. He has found a better solution to the birth trauma than anybody else. He takes revenge, breaking the thighs and killing the impure Philistines with it. He outdoes woman, making the gap acceptably large. Not only does he kill the woman and with her, her people; he makes her superfluous, too. Naastepad also establishes a link between the temple and the woman. Determined as he is to idealize Samson, he interprets the final scene as union with the beloved woman (72). He fails to explain, however, how this interpretation can be accommodated into his previous interpretations, which contradict it.

Samson has outdone and undone woman. No wonder he dies satisfied.

No wonder that, after his long travels to alien women, he is now fetched back by his male blood relatives. "Then his brethren and all the house of his father came down and took him." Now he is allowed into the country of the circumcised, the pure, the lust-free. Now the pact with God, the male principle, has finally been realized.

Who Is Samson?

Samson can be viewed as a prototype, not of the fatherly hero but of a typical category of man that emerges at a specific moment in the history of our culture. That type can be described with the help of Samson's portrait, as it has taken shape in the course of this analysis. The kernel is that *Samson is insecure in his sexuality.*

—He is conceived without sex.
—He moves into the house of a woman as often as three times.
—He keeps his masculinity a secret.
—His sexual power is in his hair, a symbol of female appeal.
—He has a special pact with the male God, actualized in a vow of purity.
—He has no children.
—His love is defined according to the feminine principle of surrender.
—He ends without woman.

One possible interpretation of this portrait could be that Samson takes an extremely long time to fight the struggle that any man has to fight between the two sides of the bisexual personality. His final choice for an exclusive relationship with men attains its climax at the very moment of the womanless birth, and therefore in relation to the feminine. His choice is a negative one: he chooses the masculine *against* women.

Fear and the desire for return to the mother's womb lead to a strong death drive. Death is, in this view, an ultimate and effective return to the mother (earth). This desire-fear complex is crossed by a struggle between active and passive impulses. For this struggle, too, Samson's death offers an appropriate solution. He dies actively by letting himself be captured passively. His passive tendency, symbolized by the full surrender he allows others to demand of him, is not resisted; he opposes it by first living it out completely. It is only after having been completely reduced to passivity that he is able to be properly socially active. The text insists that his death is his greatest performance. It realizes his ideal of unity by combining birth and death, destruction and social benefit, in a creative regression. He not only combines contradictory impulses, he also combines the individual and the social, the public welfare. If Samson is a hero, he is so because he manages to overcome the initial impossibility of reconciling these opposite interests, which were, for him, contradictions.

The actantial analysis referred at first reading to a struggle between two male forces, both *destinateurs*. At the beginning of the Delilah episode, the Philistines were the incentive; at the end, Samson was the arbiter. The double *destinateur* weakens the position of the subject. But how can we speak of struggle, if the loser is so cooperative? No real struggle then, but not as much masculinity as we might think either. The uncertain position of the actantial *destinateur* refers to a second level of meaning. There we see another subject: Samson himself, who pursues his own repressed object. That object is, then, to gain clear insight into his own sexuality. Delilah is now no more a subject of her own but a *destinateur*. Together with her Philistine blood relations, the uncircumcised, she represents the "impure," feminine side, the side of lust. She represents the drive that put Samson on a trail that fills him with fear.

The Philistines now receive a clear meaning. They represent the feminine. On the other side, and at the end of the episode, is the masculine, occupying the arbiter position. That side is represented by God, in the pact with the male God. This struggle between the Philistines and God excludes Delilah as a decisive power. She acts on orders. Hence, she loses her actantial position but at the same time her guilt. The real, unconscious struggle in Samson himself limits the number of actantially functional actors even more. God may be interpreted as an aspect of Samson's personality. The Philistines are, of course, historically "real," but they are, in the portrayal of this inner conflict, first and foremost representatives. Like Delilah, they help Samson to acquire insight into himself. This way, Samson's circle narrows more and more. Indeed, he ends up in total solitude, confronted with himself alone: circling around and around in prison. It is only after he has been locked up there long enough, a stretch of time that is represented by the growing of his hair, that he is sufficiently "purified" to lend his Naziritism a personal content. In the pact with God, in his choice for the exclusively masculine, he finds the strength to bring about autogenesis.

The other narratological problems now receive an explanation. Samson's view is not given; focalization is denied to him. First, this is because he has no view, at least not one that is clear to himself. His unconscious view is expressed by Delilah, who loses her second subjective power since she is not an independent focalizer. She only helps him to focalize and to speak. So the view at stake *is* after all Samson's. Delilah holds a mirror up to him, the mirror that, according to Lacan, allows the subject to discover and thus to constitute himself.

There is also a question about the textual level. Why does Samson not speak? Why does he only react and not take the initiative of speech? It is again the psychoanalytical framework that allows us to find an answer. The discursive situation is comparable to the analytical situation. In psychoanalysis there is a constant competition between the narrative and the dramatic mode. Self-analysis is impossible because the monologue is not dramatic, since it does not force the division of roles that is needed for transference. Delilah's role could ultimately be compared to the analyst's. It is only when she reproaches Samson for not feeling real love in the sense of surrender that he realizes that surrender is what he seeks, that he understands the real nature of his love and the anxiety that knowledge evokes in him. She is the instrument of, or the partner in, his talking cure.

Samson, Patriarchy, and Social Reality

In the course of the preceding polemical interpretation, I have tried to argue that the sample readers have been less preoccupied with the text than with the problems it poses for them. Hence, even if one wishes to agree with their view of women, one must admit that they failed to meet the criteria of adequacy and plausibility. In my turn, I have tried to show how I related my interpretation to the text, enhancing its details and its problematic aspects. The remaining question is that of relevance. It must be answered within the framework of my purpose: to account for the sexual politics involved in the text and the readings it provokes, and the importance of that issue for today's society. Such far-reaching questions cannot, of course, be answered in full here. I leave it to the reader to evaluate the whole enterprise at the end of this book. Here, I briefly outline the meaning of the myth of Samson.

What is now the meaning of this myth about the strongest man on earth? The recipients all insist on "love" as the first meaning. Naastepad does his best to see a fine, commendable love in Samson's behavior, and he skillfully circumvents contradiction by insisting on Samson's desire rather than his performance. Identifying Delilah and Samson, he seems sensitive to the homosexual tendencies, without, of course, ever naming them. That love is the main theme is obvious. The fact that it is problematized is, however, repressed, and only apparent at the painful moments when the recipients contradict their own interpretations and deviate from their initial position in order to save Samson's heroism.

The myth is, however, concerned with the *problems* of love in the first place. It is the myth of anxiety. Fear of the female, the feminine attraction and impurity, fear of initiation, of the first time. Fear of the *vagina dentata.* Fear of emotional surrender, of too strong an attachment. Fear of old age and of the return to the womb, of the powerlessness of the child. Above all, fear caused by the irresistible attraction of all these things. "Redeem us from love" is the theme of this myth, a theme that we find in many texts, from feminist novels to Napoleon's poems. These fears lead to the problematic but familiar inhibitions that make life so difficult for many of us. The emotional inhibitions are expressions of a personal, often unconscious meaning-complex that can be visualized in an incomplete semiotic square:

This diagram shows a rather frequent masculine view of woman. It is incomplete, because the diagonal disjunctions are impossible to establish. The desired freedom entails confinement, and confinement is dangerous. So a vicious triangle arises, short-circuiting freedom.

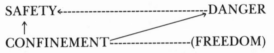

This short circuit is the space where the regressive person is trapped, like Samson, in circularity.

If the story of Samson and Delilah can be read in this way, it is no wonder that it appeals so strongly to modern readers. It does, then, mediate between the insecurities of the son-hero in early patriarchy, who represents the insecurities of the system itself, and the modern insecurities of the defensive ideology of failing patriarchy. The difference, again, has fallen in-between. Where the biblical hero displays the problems of his own subjectivity, using the female other to reach awareness, modern male readers fail to acknowledge the problematic that their "paternalized" hero cannot afford in his new status. The insecurity is projected onto the outside figure of the other: the woman.

There is no point in evaluating the degree of "patriarchity" of the two accounts of the Samson story, the ancient and the modern. There is difference, and the difference concerns the position of the woman. It also concerns the man, the hero that represents male values and male concerns. The repression of the insecurity in the older text results in a deprivation of the modern reader. Denying the need for expression, the overly secure rewriters deny their audience the benefit of Samson's talking cure. This is not to suggest that the biblical text is more gynophilic. It is patriarchal in other ways. It is, for example, male-centered to the extreme: Delilah gradually lost all her subject-positions in the course of my reading. It represses the woman and enhances the man. But doing so, it cannot but betray what it tries to get rid of: the insecurity such a repression entails. The repressed returns differently in the modern versions: Delilah is, there, the utterly important, albeit lethal, woman. Between those two forms of repression and return, emphatically different, I do not wish to choose.

·3·

HEROISM AND PROPER NAMES, OR THE FRUITS OF ANALOGY

Balancing the Tension

Once the underlying passivity and fears of impotence of heroes like David the Great and Samson the Strong are plausible, and once the procedures of ideological transformations as they are displayed in both scholarly and popular reception are outlined, the insecurity in patriarchal heroism can be studied in its artistic figuration. It is time to examine in more detail the typical narrative art of the biblical love stories and the way that art exposes specific attitudes toward sexuality. Such a study cannot be comprehensive and there is no need for it to be. My aim is not to describe biblical narrative art and differentiate it from modern Western literature as, for example, Robert Alter does (1981); rather, I wish to point to the ideological changes brought about by these differences insofar as the relations between the sexes are concerned. Therefore I will analyze only one feature that I consider basic. In the next three chapters, character production and the representational devices involved, especially the attitudes toward chronology, will be the focus.

Literary characters, as representations, as images of the culturally valid view of the subject, have the property of displaying, in condensed form, the problematics inherent in that view. As will become clear in the last chapter, a specific and in some sense alien tension between analogy and chronology is characteristic of biblical love stories. It is that very tension which facilitates the evolution of the myths from one culture to another. Understanding of that tension from within is a first condition of its neutralization.

In this chapter, the construction of characters in the Book of Ruth will be approached from the point of view of the function of proper names. That construction is dependent on a device that falls under the general heading of *analogy*. The proper name and its narrative function reveal, however, the fact that analogy can work only within a concept of chronology. The interdependence of both allows only relative differentiation.

They are delicately balanced, and a fruitful understanding of text and reception is based on a flexible view of their dynamic relation. Once the importance of analogy as a function of typically biblical metatextuality is established, the limits of too strict a thematic reading must be demonstrated. To that end, the same device will be considered from the point of view of a dialectic of chronology in chapter 4.

In the Book of Ruth, characters can only be heroes insofar as they resemble one another. At first sight, this collective heroism is alien to our notion of individualism, but it becomes self-evident as soon as the use of the text in Jewish liturgy is brought into consideration. Using the terminology of modern literary theory, I wish to show that this mode of reading is not as radically novel as it may seem. The document of reception that serves as a starting point is, this time, a piece of creative writing. It will not demonstrate ideological misreading as did the rewritings in the previous chapters. The case is more complex. As I argued earlier, distortions are unavoidable, but the particular orientation they choose is relatively optional. Victor Hugo's poem features here the possibility of ideological variation: although his poem is not without connections to the general modern view of sexuality, it is based on aspects of the biblical book that have remained unnoticed in Christian reception, buried as the story has been under morality and the need for male, individual heroism.

Starting from a Detail

Sa barbe était d'argent comme un ruisseau d'avril
Sa gerbe n'était point avare ni haineuse
Quand il voyait passer quelque pauvre glaneuse:
"Laissez tomber exprès des épis," disait-il.

His beard was silver like a spring brook
his sheaf was neither miserly nor spiteful.
When he saw some poor gleaner passing by
he said: "drop ears on purpose."

Hugo's poem, which is part of *La légende des siècles* (1859), uses the story of Ruth in an evocation of an old man's mysterious experience of love on a peaceful summer night. In an attempt to make the elements of the story more general, Hugo interestingly reverses the perspective. Thus he draws attention to a reversal in the text itself.

The quoted verses are the best-known lines of Hugo's poem "Booz endormi." They have been commented upon by Jacques Lacan (1966) and, subsequently, by Anne Ubersfeld (1974) and Michel Grimaud (1978).

The first feature of the poem that strikes the reader is the choice of the male character as the protagonist. In most commentaries on the Book of Ruth, Boaz is interpreted as the *destinateur*: it is the generous Boaz, who, from the height of his position as a rich man, allows the "pauvre gla-neuse" Ruth to reach her goal, so well deserved: a place of her own, under the roof of some rich man.

Lacan, in a most convincing metatext, directs attention to the funda-mental negativity of Hugo's poem, in which the proclaimed generosity of the man is questionable. "Sa générosité affirmée se voit réduite à moins que rien par la munificence de la gerbe qui, d'être prise à la nature, ne connaît pas notre réserve et nos rejets" (His explicit generosity is reduced to less than nothing by the richness of the sheaf which, taken from nature, is ignorant of our reservations and rejections) (507). And Gri-maud writes in his commentary on Lacan: "En effet, un des aspects qu'on a toujours négligés lors de la lecture de 'Booz,' c'est l'intensité des pro-testations d'impuissance" (Indeed, one of the aspects always neglected in readings of 'Booz' is the intensity of the affirmations of impotence) (1978: 103).

It is difficult indeed, to close one's eyes to the sexual meaning, and this in a negative sense, of the verse in which Uebersfeld (1974:587) sees a paradigmatic example of the shift from metonymy (Boaz and the sheaf he possesses) to metaphor (Boaz and the sheaf he *is*). I would suggest that synecdoche is the means of this transition. It is only because Boaz considers the sheaf as a significant part of himself that it can take its metaphorical meaning.

The fabula of the Book of Ruth is well known: on the advice of Naomi, her mother-in-law, Ruth goes in her finest dress to try to seduce Boaz into a marriage that would protect both impoverished women from mis-ery. The seduction attempt is incredibly outspoken and daring: by night, the young widow takes her place in Boaz's bed, uncovers his feet (if not "worse": the Hebrew word is ambiguous and also means "testicles") in order to "lay by him." Even the most moralizing and orthodox commen-taries refrain from attempting to "cover up" the sensational story and engage in a more promising strategy: they try to defend Ruth's move as understandable, to naturalize it and thus to make it morally acceptable.

Lacan and Grimaud, both sensitive to the old Hugoesque Boaz's anxi-ety, his fear of dying childless, are interested in the *displacement* in the tenth verse of the French poem ("sa gerbe n'était point avare ni hai-neuse"), which transforms the shocking metaphor into an innocent meton-ymy, without entirely succeeding in the repression of ambiguity, still preserved in the possessive adjective "sa." *Displacement,* that fundamental figure of Freudian rhetoric and that most efficient tool of censorship, is manifest not only on the microstructural level of this verse and its rhetorical figure of speech. In this chapter, I want to deal not with the displacement the poem contains, but with the one it *constitutes, is,* and this in the most concrete sense of the word. Thus the transition from metonymy via synecdoche to metaphor characterizes not only Hugo's verse but also its relation to the biblical book and even, as will become clear, the composition of the book itself. Indeed, compared to the biblical book, Hugo's poem is the result of the maximizing of a detail, a telephoto effect. The detail is a short fragment of the seduction scene (Ruth 3:6–16). The enlarging, which, as with any synecdoche, necessarily entails displacement, is two-sided. First, the poet picks out a secondary character to make him the protagonist of his version of the fabula. Second, the detail he picks in the whole scene is a motif that is hardly explicit, the one of verse 10: "Blessed be thou of the Lord, my daughter: for thou hast shewed more kindness in the latter end than at the beginning, inasmuch as thou followest not young men, whether poor or rich."

As opposed to nonliterary metatexts, that is, theological commentaries or works of literary scholarship, the poem stresses feelings that this verse only touches upon: Boaz's fear of old age, of losing his sexual potency and attractiveness, of being incapable of changing his sad situation as a childless widower. In the poem, the enormous oak that, in his dream, grows out of his belly, loaded with posterity, constitutes the image, moving in its directness, of the rich man's worries. From that point of view, Ruth's approach is a stroke of luck that he would not have dared to hope for and, indeed, he is most grateful to her for she will help him out of *his* misery. The whole development of Hugo's poem comes out of this verse, as vital for the poem as is the oak for Boaz. Not only, then, does Hugo displace emphases; he totally reverses the perspective. He changes the story of Boaz's generosity into that of Ruth's generosity, and he changes the very meaning of the concept: while Boaz gave what he possessed, Ruth gives what she *is*.

Two assimilations produce Hugo's figuration of Boaz's dream. In the Christian exegetic tradition, a confusion often exists between Boaz's and Jesse's tree. This can be seen, for example, on the windows of the Chartres cathedral. A second confusion, for which Hugo may not have had any source, is the one between this tree and another "erection," the ladder also seen in a dream, by Jacob. The condensation is revealing, based as it is on dreams of election, ascension, and posterity as one and the same issue. Hugo's representation of Boaz's dream of potency enhances the conception of individual male success as a position in history. At the same time, it opens up the difference between what one *is* and where one *stands*, between one's position in analogy and in chronology, which ultimately differentiates between the book as a love story and as history.

Even the most feminist of commentaries, Phyllis Trible's classic analysis (1978), does not account for the problematic aspect of verse 3:10 in terms of coherence. Indeed, Trible's interpretation stresses, like most scholarly metatexts, the idyllic side of the Book of Ruth, with which the quoted verse is so violently in contradiction. On the other hand, works of art conceived after this source text give a more interesting account of possible readings. Hugo's poem is not the only one. We know Rembrandt's painting *The Jewish Bride,* which is sometimes claimed to represent Ruth and Boaz. Here, Boaz is depicted putting his hand on Ruth's breast, an obviously sexual gesture. Instead of sticking to a paraphrasing critique of the text, which cannot go beyond overtly stated meanings, according to which Ruth's happiness in finding a solvent husband is the well-deserved price for her devotion to her old mother-in-law, and according to which, consequently, Boaz remains a pale figure as the *destinateur* in the background, and can easily be recuperated as prefiguring Christ, it seems more interesting first to take the status of the book seriously. The Book of Ruth is an institutionalized *metatext,* which was meant to be read at specific feasts and to comment upon the Torah.

Commenting upon Ruth, Hugo provides a cue to take the story as comment upon the Torah. If in Hugo's version the female name has disappeared from the title, we should not mistake that change, for that displacement helps to illuminate another displacement, of which the last half of verse 3:10 only displays a trace. Displacing the displacement, then, Hugo reinstates the repressed side of the text, which is its metatextual function in the first place. The question then arises: what is the content of the commentary that the book is supposed to give?

In verse 3:10, there was a kindness at stake. The word is an understatement—most translations give "generosity." The kindness alluded to was a kindness "in the beginning." There is a first kindness, and then there is a second kindness, evaluated as greater. The latter kindness, and thus the best one, is Ruth's courting of Boaz. The first one, discussed several times already, is spoken about for the first time at the end of chapter 1: "And Ruth clave unto her" (1:14). Now, this verb is a very strong one. It is used in Gen. 2:24 to say that man will cleave unto his wife. It is exclusively used with a male subject, in reference to the matrimonial bond. Also, it is active, signifying the free choice made by a subject to renounce freedom in favor of another being. With these features of the verb in mind, it is easy to evaluate as an instance of censorship the translation of the *Alliance Biblique Française,* which runs: "Mais Ruth refusa de se séparer d'elle," where the verb "refuser," by its inherent negativity, undermines the subject's position as active, and its action as positive adherence.

Ruth's faithfulness to Naomi or, we may say more directly, her *love* for Naomi, is praised several times, and by Boaz himself in 2:11–12. Her generosity, compared with which this legendary love almost vanishes, consists, according to Boaz, in her not "following young men." The scandal of the comparison is more audible in the artistic sensibility of both Hugo and Rembrandt than in the censored rationalism of scholarly metatexts or in "purified" rewritings like children's Bibles. Ann Edwards, for example, replaces the comparison with a sheer juxtaposition: "For you have not looked at the young men, rich or poor, and you have remained with your mother-in-law" (1969:196). The Hebrew technically allows, of course, a juxtaposition, but juxtaposition itself easily signifies a comparison. It is, however, impossible not to take this scandal into account, because without it the verse simply doesn't make sense. I would even go so far as to assume that either the comparison *is* strikingly scandalous or the verse is a corruption of the text. Even the most moralistic metatexts have not gone that far.

Let us take the hypertrophy of the detail and relate it to the text, on the one hand, and to Hugo's metatextual reversal, on the other. It is, then, a *symptom*, in both Peirce's general and Freud's specific sense. The displacement is a displacement of a displacement. We will shortly see how the texts on which Ruth comments form a chain of samples of sexual relations that Ruth criticizes and represses in the same move. Thus the metatextual aspects of the book hide their own revolutionary import, allowing, without forcing it, a patriarchal reception. What is revolutionary is, as I will argue shortly, the possibility of the construction of Boaz as a hero through metatextual identification with female characters. This construction, which we will now turn to, operates through the narrative exploitation of the proper name.

Narrativization of the Proper Name

More often than not, biblical names have a meaning. If they don't have one, they are assigned one in the text's afterlife. Far from being sheerly deictic, like names in today's Western culture, they have a specific meaning that integrates the character into its life, and that can also imprison it there. The name *Orpah*, for example, given to the character of contrast who in Ruth 1:14 follows the advice of her mother-in-law to privilege the reality principle and return to her family in order to find a husband among her own people, means "back" or "neck," and is explained by Midrash Rabbah: "because she turned her back" (1977). Hence the meaning that became standard: "The one who turns the neck." Not only is the name in such cases so well adapted to the character that we could say that it is iconic rather than symbolic, keeping its indexical aspect; it is also narrative. For, far from describing just a feature of the character, it tells its action—an emblematic action, indeed, which thus becomes predictive, but which remains narrated action. This entails the problem of chronology and its relation to analogy.

Receiving the name, the little girl was not yet "the one who turns the neck," but she was already defined as such. She is subjected to her name, determined by it. It is because she has this name that she will remain her whole life "the one who turns the neck," until history will finally allow her to do what is expected from her. Lacan would have here a good example of his concept of the subject subjected to the symbolic order as early as before birth, by the proper name. The model, of which Orpah is our paradigm case, also contains a statement on narrative discourse. In biblical culture, the word and the thing are not separated, and we don't need to insist on the importance of the Verb for the creation of the world that Yahweh wished to be so thoroughly semiotic. The narrative order articulates and models this world, and Orpah, charged with her narrative role as abandoner and her semantic content as the opposite of Ruth the faithful, had no way of defending herself against the destiny that order assigned to her by analogy.

Things are not always so fatal. The character is not completely defenseless against the name. Naomi the sweet, for example, bitter because of the accumulaton of misery that befalls her, chooses the name of Mara the bitter one, deciding to call things by their names. History may dominate the subject; at least the latter can face the situation, assume the focalization of its own life. But Naomi, however justified her decision may seem at the moment she makes it, does not take the narrativity of her name into account. For within the narrative order, it is the case that if she has the name of Naomi the sweet, that is because, sooner or later, she will be Naomi the sweet. The name, which seems to have become irrelevant at a certain point, has not lost its predictive force.

Summarizing the lives of characters, names interpret them. Among all the events that could befall Orpah, it is her separation from Naomi—the choice it implies and the elimination of the character from the book when she turns her neck, disappears from Naomi's life—that the name reveals. The character is summarized by her name; so is the text devoted to that name.

In the case of Naomi, chronology corrects analogy. History corrects the character who had not enough faith in her name. Hence, there is a metatextual aspect in proper names. It is related to their iconic aspect: it operates through it. In modern literature, we have cases of semanticized names. The meanings we have seen in the names of Bovary and Homais, the "barres raides" in the name of the husband Desbaresdes in *Moderato Cantabile,* are elements of a significant semantic network. But as distinct from those cases, aspects of names in Ruth *tell.* And since they can only tell the crucial, determining action, by which the destiny of the character is summarized, the bond they make between chronology and analogy comes close to what the French call a *mise en abyme*, a microstructure that contains a summary of the overall fabula in which it functions (Dällen-bach 1977; Bal 1986; Jefferson 1983). To use Shoshana Felman's terms, when she deals with the idea of paternity (1980): "C'est un promesse de *sens* propre et de nom *propre*" (It is a promise of proper *meaning* and of *proper* name).

Boaz's name means the powerful/potent. Naming him so, the text comments upon its own fabula from a point of view that is opposed to Victor Hugo's. But Hugo deals with names differently. He integrates the names of his characters into another network, which has a complexity of its own. He picks the name of the male character for his title. Now, the Book of Ruth is one of only two books in the Hebrew Bible that have women's names as their titles. Should we suppose that Hugo the male could not stand all this attention being given to the woman? Not at all. For he adds the word "endormi," as if he wanted both to draw our attention to the hypertrophy of the woman in the biblical context in which she otherwise has a definitely minor role to play, *and* to suggest an interpretation for it: it is *because* Boaz is sleeping that the woman can take this initiative. Boaz the powerful/potent is, in fact, Boaz the sleeper, the weak, the impotent. The sleep of the male is seen as a *sine qua non* of woman's access to her femininity.

The textual problem raised retrospectively by Hugo's metatext is symmetrical to the other textual problem of the Book of Ruth, found in the middle of chapter 4, verses 11 and 12. This detail is part of the narration of a scene that goes from verse 1 to verse 12 and that is the only scene of the book in which there is no woman. In this passage, proper names are used in another way, with more explicit metatextuality. It is probably not by coincidence that the problem is even constituted by the proper name. The contrast between this scene and the previous one is systematic. There, the fabula was played out during the night, in the warmest intimacy, in Boaz's bed. Here, the following sequence is in public, at the city gate, the place of jurisdiction—the place, too, that separates the female from the male domain. It is the entry point of the city. The action consists of a trial—the trial by which Boaz will legally acquire Ruth—men's business, exclusively, while the object, the price at stake, is a woman.

Jurisdiction is basically a commentary on the law. Hence the metatextual character of the scene. In this process, the elders of the city evoke a few proper names, the narrative content of which stretches far beyond the occasion for which they are summoned. We can even assume that the knowledge that the elders (in other words, the authorities) can possibly have of the motive for the allusion is insufficient to justify it. For the only motive can be analogy: the presumed iconicity between the cases evoked and the case at stake. I quote the problematic verses:

> The Lord make the woman that is come into thine house like Rachel and like Leah, which did build the house of Israel . . .
> 12 And let thy house be like the house of Pharez, whom Tamar bare unto Judah, of the seed which the Lord shall give thee of this young woman.

Let me first draw attention to the fact that the use of the proper name is not only more explicitly metatextual but also more explicitly narrative. For the name goes with the narration of actions of which the evoked women are the subjects: in other words, childbearing, realizing the dream of the enormous oak. Building the house of Israel: the Hebrew Bible being, to some extent, entirely consecrated to that construction, we come close to a totalizing *mise en abyme,* which would contain not only the texts directly alluded to (Genesis 30 and 38) but the Torah as a whole and even, by extension, the Bible as a whole, including the past and future fabulae it contains. The difference between analogy and chronology is almost ruled out.

The textual problem raised is the irrelevance of the two evocations. "Rachel and Leah" form a strange doubling of the woman Ruth. We shall have to examine their case in order to understand to what extent the elders are rather over-relevant. The allusion to Tamar is overtly painful. She bore her son Parez unto the old Judah, her father-in-law, and the role of the male, in that story, is far from edifying, as will become clear in the next chapter. To evoke her to the old Boaz, anxious to possess a young woman legally, in obedience to the rules of the society, in spite of the insecurity he had expressed to her only, the previous night, seems a displaced and indiscreet allusion that is not very reassuring. It is difficult to imagine that the elders, who are so much in favor of the solution Boaz proposes, would deliberately try to hurt him.

There is a third name in this scene, the thrice-pronounced name of Moab, Ruth's country. This country is no other than the country of Moab, the son of Lot, whom Lot engendered with his own daughter, unaware and during his drunkard's sleep. We will have to return to that synecdochical name too. Together, the names evoked in this scene form a series that is indeed narrowly tied up with "the building of the house of Israel," with the relations between the sexes and procreation. Taken together, the names form a *mise en abyme par excellence*: the *mise en abyme* that, instead of proposing one interpretation, as is usually the case, offers all possibilities.

Since the problems evoked have to do with narrative subjects, with social life and unconscious allusions, I will briefly follow the three lines such an account suggests: narratological, historical, and psychoanalytical analyses.

In Search of the Subject

It may seem useless, in a text where the female character is appointed heroine as early as the title itself, to try and account for her place in the subjectivity of the text. The structure of the latter is less simple than it seems at first sight, however. For, as we have seen in the previous chapters, the overall subjectivity in a text is not accounted for solely by the one character who is the hero or heroine. The number of speeches allotted to each character in the Book of Ruth is tallied in Table 5. Obviously, there is no self-evident reason to privilege Ruth. Naomi speaks often, and the order of speech acts shows that she takes the initiative, while Ruth reacts. Ruth executes Naomi's projects, if in a somewhat autonomous way. In the middle section Boaz takes a few initiatives, too. His addresses belong to the public domain: he speaks to the elders, to his employees, and he speaks privately and publicly to Ruth. The collective speakers are remarkable. Their function is thoroughly social. They react to and comment upon events, representing, as does the chorus in classical tragedy, public opinion. The first collective speaker consists of the inhabitants of Bethlehem, who verbalize, in the interrogative form, Naomi's pain, revealing—but interrogatively—the contradiction between the name and the character, thus between the word and the thing, a contradiction that is inconceivable. Therefore, Naomi does not accept being publicly named as something that she is not.

In the last chapter there are two distinct collective speakers, each speaking twice. First the elders speak, then the neighbors of Naomi. They are the last quoted speaker; they have the last word.

Table 5

Chapter	1	2	3	4
Narrator	3	7	3	7
Naomi	4	4	2	0
Ruth	2	5	3	0
Boaz	0	5	3	4
Redeemer	—	—	—	3
Collective Speaker	1	0	0	4

In the action of this book, focalization is at stake. How are we to see
Naomi's situation? We have noticed already that she corrects the view
expressed by her name. How are we to see in the first chapter the situation of her daughters-in-law? Three visions are given, implicitly or explicitly. Naomi gives her evaluation first; the two women oppose hers;
finally, Orpah takes over Naomi's view, while Ruth perseveres. Boaz,
when he first sees Ruth, asks information about her. When the information is positive, but only then, he takes on himself the favorable view of
Ruth. How are we to see Boaz's project? He asks the elders. He does not
know that Naomi has given her view already and that he is left merely to
act it out. The two middle chapters contain many questions, wishes,
promises. If Naomi is once mistaken about her own life, Ruth never is.
Boaz is not either, but for another reason: as we have seen, he develops
his view as derived from the public view. However, as supreme proof of
his subjective power, he dares add one view of his own: the one expressed in 3:10.

So far the textual subjectivity has been shared mainly by two elder
characters, Boaz and Naomi. Ruth's subject position, however autonomous it sometimes seems to be, is formally derived from the two elders.
Naomi is privileged; her activities frame those of Boaz. The analysis of
the fabula does not add much to this picture. Actions are neatly separated, and each character has his or her share. Naomi takes initiatives in
the private domain, Boaz in the public sphere. It is striking, however,
that Boaz's initiatives need social support from other subjects. After his
first encounter with Ruth, he asks for information about her, as if he
wants to make sure that any eventual move on his side will be sanctioned
beforehand. The trial at the gate exemplifies this need. Naomi's and
Ruth's behavior is opposed to Boaz's: they brave public opinion.

Here the evocations by the elders intervene. Speakers of authority,
they carry out the performative act of wishing, a lighter form of promise—lighter precisely in terms of its lack of authority. The elders, however powerful they may be, cannot completely determine what the subject Ruth will do or be. They do not master chronology but do something
else instead. They evoke, by analogy, three other women, subjects of the
building of the house of Israel, thus sanctioning a sexual practice in
which the power of the male is overruled by the female subject.

This brief analysis of narratological subject positions emphasizes the
following points. Subjectivity is not, by priority, assigned to Ruth. Naomi
has a place of honor, but not exclusively. There is repartition, the different domains of life being functions of that repartition. Boaz is as
important a subject as Naomi, but he is less autonomous. He needs help.
Surprised by Ruth's unexpected presence, he "is afraid" (3:8). We can
see a fairly spectacular sign of the derivative nature of his power in the

fact that, in spite of his awareness of the return and misery of his kins-woman Naomi, he does nothing to help her.

Ruth reaches full textual subjectivity in the metatext only. The meta-text is prospective, in the performed wish that can be realized in the future only, and that precisely will not be realized. For the child Obed that she will bear will be born to Naomi. At the same time, the wish is retrospective, in the equation it establishes between Ruth and the three women of the past. This double temporal aspect is significant: the present is lacking.

In Search of Foundations, or the Subjects versus the Law

In order to evaluate Boaz's subject position as compared with that of the other characters, we have to take a look at the institution to which he addresses himself in his insecurity: the law. The law functions as the center of the different social and economical problems around which this fabula is turning, and if one wants to avoid anachronistic interpretation, this situation cannot be ignored. The law specifies the relations between the characters, first of all between male and female, but also between generations, and it sets the limits to individual freedom. The very fact that those limits are thematized is a sign; it gives evidence of a specific attitude toward legitimacy and transgression.

The law, the institutions in relation to which the subject establishes itself (Lacan), is at the same time the paradoxical institution that both sets the limits to subjectivity and, by its fundamentally *intersubjective* nature, *subject* to interpretation by *subjects* who are *subjected* to it, designs the limits of its own (pseudo-) objectivity. It represents the performative acts of interdiction (of transgression) and of promise (of social intersubjectivity), both turned toward the future; it also represents the constative act of *stating* (transgression in the past). Once more, the present is lacking, and when the present is lacking, the subject is alone.

That the problem raised in this text is social in the first place is already obvious when we consider the systematic opposition between the charac-ters. Ruth is badly off: she is a woman, a widow, a foreigner, and child-less. Her tribe lives in hostility with the Jews (Num. 25). Naomi is not a foreigner, but she is a childless widow, and too old to change that situa-tion. At the other side of the opposition we have Boaz. He is a male, rich, and he lives on his own land. He is an ideal citizen: constantly aware of morality (2:11; 3:12–13), of law (4:1–12), and of formal justice, he may qualify, with only a little anachronism, as an *honnête homme*. Ruth's and Naomi's problems are economic. Boaz represents the possession that is opposed to their hunger (his sheaf). But their problems are chronological as well, in that the line of history is threatened by their childless widowhood. Boaz, as we have seen, has the same problem, and so the neat opposition is broken. This little unevenness provides an entrance into the problem, a "brèche vers une latence" (breach toward a latency), as Delay phrased it in his study of Gide, which develops around the tension between laws. Indeed, there is a tension between the letter and the spirit of the law. Each one of the main characters has a problem to settle with the law. Let us see how they choose their approaches.

The first conflict is mentioned in verse 1:16. Ruth defies Yahweh himself. In Deut. 23:2–4, her tribe had been excluded from Yahweh's congregation unto the tenth generation. There is a double motive for this exclusion. In Deuteronomy it is said that the Moabites had not fed the Israelites when they were starving in the desert. But in Num. 25:1 a second reason is given: the sons of Israel had relations with the daughters of Moab: "illegal cleaving," we could say. Fortunately, Yahweh will take Ruth's side. For in spirit she *is* a daughter of Israel. She deliberately chose the insecure position of a foreign widow out of solidarity (*ḥesed*) with her mother-in-law, who advised the opposite. Thereby she has earned the right of transgression, so that the laws of Israel do apply to her, as we see in 4:5.

The second tension between law and legitimacy is more problematic. It is the tension between the law of *gōēl* and the law of levirate. The law of *gōēl* obliges the closest kinsman of an impoverished woman to redeem the land that that person is forced to sell. The law provides a sort of social security, and is at the same time a means of preventing alienation of property from the family. The law of levirate obliges the brother of a dead man to marry the widow if she has no children. This law has two sides to it, as well: it protects the widows and, probably in the first place, insures posterity for the dead. For the child born of that union will be named after the dead. This law is thematized in Genesis 38 and will be discussed in the next chapter.

In verse 4:6 the unnamed kinsman refuses to marry Ruth, though he had been ready to redeem the land. Juridically speaking, this man is in the right. For he is not her brother-in-law. The confusion of both laws would be a transgression of another law, the one of Deut. 22:22 and following: the law against illegal "cleaving." The not very clear relation between the law of *gōēl* and the law of levirate (Lev. 25:23 and following, versus Deut. 25:5) would make the man transgress the taboo of Deut. 22:22 and following and that of Deut. 23:2. The cheap moralism of many commentaries that blame this man for being interested only in acquiring land and pursuing his personal interests points to the evolution from biblical to Christian attitudes. It hides the deeper problems involved. For again, the apparent opposition between the two characters,

Boaz and the unnamed man, goes together with resemblance. As Hugo showed us in his account of verse 3:10, Boaz also has an interest of his own. Being already rich, the interest is just different. Second, Boaz *wishes* the unnamed man to refrain from his right to *gōēl*. That wish is the very reason why he does not call him by his name: he wants him, at all costs, not to marry Ruth, not to enter into the legal system in which subjects have intersubjective names. Also, he does not give all the information right away. Third, since the man seeks, like Boaz, to establish his subjectivity in the law, there is no reason to blame the one rather than the other. Like a mirror image of Orpah, he obeys the reality principle. If he is to blame, it would be at most for being a little formalistic, like one of those people who in meetings are eager to talk about rules and procedures in order to delay the fearful moment of dealing with the matter at hand. If he were to be completely wrong, there would be no tension in the story, which would then be a simplistic story of the victory of good over evil. Moralism hidden in an idyll—that is what most commentaries make of it. Thus they destroy it. For if there is tension, it is *because* this man is right. It is because, indeed, Boaz is in danger of transgressing the law of Deut. 22:22. The ambiguous scene on the threshing floor, which Hugo's poem emphasized, is the climax of that tension. What happens there is not only that Ruth uncovers Boaz's feet and/or sexual parts, that Boaz wakes up and is afraid, that he asks the woman at his feet *who* she is, and not, as in 2:5, *whose* she is, but also that he praises her, being full of gratitude to her for choosing him and not a young man who, not only rich but even poor, would in Boaz's eyes be far more attractive to her than he is.

The tension between the two laws is inherent in the two domains they cover, which are not unrelated. *Gōēl* is the law of the possession of land; levirate concerns posterity. These two aspects constitute history. That they do is exactly one of the messages that the book of Ruth, where they are constantly mixed, delivers.

When Naomi leaves her country during the period of starvation, for example, she has children (she is "full"), but she has no food. In Moab, the country of fertility, but also the country of promiscuity, she receives food but loses her children. She returns "empty." Back in Bethlehem, she has nothing. The strictly illegal combination of *gōēl* and levirate, the law of land and the law of persons, restores both to her. Thus history moves on again, after a threat of stagnation. Therefore, law and justice, of which the latter is metatextual in relation to the former, are so crucial in this text. Therefore the trial at the gate has to be held, as the trial between law and legitimacy.

The testimony of the elders provides Boaz, the perfect citizen, the weak subject, with the indispensable support he needs to dare to transgress the law while at the same time allowing him to find the foundation of his very transgression in the law. The trial is a try-out of law itself.

We can summarize this whole field of problems in six motifs, expressed in key words, each of which brings up a social domain as regulated in some law (Table 6). The relations among all these motifs are brought to light in the scene of the trial:

      trial   testimony   justice   jurisdiction

All the problems of the concerned subjects will be solved in this event: the sexual problem of Boaz will find a solution in the solution to the economical problem of Naomi, so that together they can set history in motion again, the history of "the building of the house of Israel."

Table 6

Motif	Key Word	Social Domain	Law
same/ different	to leave/ to return	"international" relations	cursing Moab (Deut. 23:2–4; Num. 25:1)
possession	land	economy/ history	gōēl (Lev. 25:23)
posterity	child	demography/ history	levirate (Deut. 25:5)
morality	cleaving	sexuality	law against promiscuity (Deut. 22:22 and following)
hunger	empty	economy	gōēl

The Unconscious Performing Speech Acts: Symptoms

The slightly misplaced combination of laws can be considered as one of those involuntary signs that Peirce calls symptoms, and at which Freud addressed the very pointed question: symptoms of what? In Peirce's logic, the distinction between symptoms as involuntary signs, and signals as signs of which the sender is aware, seems almost a Freudian slip. Why did it matter within Peirce's typology of semiotic aspects, whether or not the sender *knew*? Freud, who was more concerned with the motivations of symptoms, since only by working through those motivations could he cure them, asked the question that Peirce could have asked, had he gone beyond logic. His logic would have gained in consistency, since the displacement of accents between sign and interpretant would have helped to differentiate further between his other types: icon, index, and symbol. We can only dream about an encounter between these two geniuses, Peirce and Freud. As it stands, symptoms remain problematic, especially in texts, where there is no sender to examine. If we agree to replace the sender with textual habits, we may arrive at some intuitions about how the two concepts of the symptom would be able to interact. We will, then, start at those signs which are characterized by the encroachment of the "a-normal" into the "normal." They are abundantly present in Ruth, and first of all in the mixture of laws.

There are other "mixtures," transgressions of clear limits, like the one between the public and the private that Ruth so blatantly transgresses when she goes back to the field where she had been gleaning the day before, only to go to the center of the field, the threshing floor, which, by a strange mixture, is also Boaz's bed. The trial at the city gate, at the entrance to the female domain, where two men debate the question of who dares to take the woman, is the *place* of the mixture. It is possible to assume that the mixtures are based on an unconscious feeling of resemblance, of analogy between two items that have been mixed up, so that the symptom can be said to be based on a form of *iconicity*.

There are also slips, *lapsus* in the classical sense. We can speak of a *lapsus* whenever a word is attributed to a woman that is "normally" exclusively attributed to a man. We have already noticed the case of the verb "to cleave" (1:14), "normally" used in relation to men and referring to heterosexual relationships. A slip that is also generally noticed, but left unexplained, is the one in verse 4:17, which is symmetrical to the former. Here again a word is "inadvertently" attributed to a woman: "There is a son born to Naomi." A lapsus of this kind stresses the tension between arbitrary and motivated signs; thus, it questions the *symbolic* (in the Peircean sense). The expression is "normally" reserved for the father. What social convention calls "normal" is supposed to be the domain of the symbolic in the Peircean sense. One remembers the Alsatian woman who found the word "Käse" so much more "natural" than "fromage." Using words in an "unnatural" way, assigning them to the "wrong" subjects, is bringing the indexical bond between the word and the group that "naturally" possesses it to the fore. This latter bond is then exposed in its arbitrariness, on a different, less innocent level than the arbitrariness of the linguistic sign. This arbitrariness of indexical monopoly is the basis of linguistic classism.

A third group of symptoms consists of *allusions* that seem to be misplaced. They are *indexical* to a larger extent than they seem to be; thus, they question the distinction between analogy and chronology. The allusions—to Rachel and Leah, to Tamar, to Moab—all refer to an earlier phase of the "building of the house of Israel"; hence they extend the fabula's chronological span, including past phases. They are also *wishes* and thus include the future. On another level, they are, however, basically analogical. It is through the analogy between the comparant and the compared that the chronological extension is possible at all. When taken together, a new chronology will establish itself. As we will see shortly, the analogies show differences, and the assessment of the differences produces the unconscious chronology of the different phases of repression of women.

The restrospective allusions, the comparisons between Ruth and other women, illuminate a paradoxical phenomenon, already touched upon in the previous chapters: a collective unconscious. For the elders can hardly be supposed to be intent upon hurting the very Boaz whose project they overtly applaud; yet they display a rather painful insight into what happened, without having any factual knowledge. We have seen the same intuitive knowledge displayed by Joab; the ideology adopted here is, however, different. Social subjects as the elders are, they do not represent the law itself. They can only refer to it; they can say how they interpret it, in relation to Boaz's interpretation. Collective speakers, they speak about the law; they *are* not the law. Their discourse is metatextual in principle. Thus they testify "juridically" but also linguistically to the inescapably (inter)subjective status of legal foundations.

What is "wrong" with these symptoms of which the elders are the speakers? The first allusion consists of a doubling of the female subject. Ruth is compared to both Rachel and Leah. The case of these two wives of Jacob is significant. Hugo responds in several ways to this allusion. The confusion between Boaz's dreamlike nocturnal adventure and the dream of Jacob's ascension becomes more interesting at this point. The analogy rests on the conflation of the sexual aspect of the one and the ambition of the other. Thus, Hugo rewrites the philosophy of history as he sees it—giving women and sexuality the credit of indispensability. We have reason enough, then, to take a closer look at the case of Jacob's wives.

The fabula is well known: Jacob wanted to marry the beautiful Rachel. He labors seven years in the service of her father, Laban, who happens to be his uncle, and at the marriage the veiled bride turns out to be the ugly Leah, substituted for her beautiful sister thanks to the invisibility of the veiled face. Jacob has to labor seven more years to deserve his beloved. This split between love and fertility, which is also that between sexuality and maternity, is only too well known. Rachel complains about her lack of children, and Leah complains about the absence of the husband, the lack of love.

The problem is solved when the two women manage, in a collaboration that materializes entirely without their husband, to conquer each other's shares by abandoning their privilege. Leah gives her sister the fruit that fertilizes (cp. the fruit of the tree that gave sexual knowledge in Genesis 2), while Rachel sends her the husband. This encouraging story rests on the efforts the two women accomplish to break out of the narrow limits set by their father and husband. The exchange is thus thoroughly subversive. The elders, in Ruth, comment upon that story by acknowledging afterwards the rightness of the women's subversion when they equate Ruth to the position of Rachel and Leah together. The equation $1 + 1 = 1$, which restores the unity of the two aspects of femininity that were separated by the men, also illuminates Boaz's position. For if, as Lacan rightly points out à propos of Hugo's poem, he was worried about his lack of posterity—his symbolic castration that Hugo adds to the story—the dream of the great oak reveals Boaz's worries about sexual impotence as well. The comparison displays not only the legitimacy of feminine subversion, but the interest man has in accepting it as well, even the interest he has in participation. Slowly, a conception of "collective heroism" comes to the fore. A new form of hero, different from both the filial and the paternal hero, emerges here.

But there is more. There is a second woman in this case as well, and, further, there is a second comparison. The second woman in the Ruth story is Naomi. The solidarity (*ḥesed*) between Ruth and Naomi gives social security and posterity to the one by means of the sexuality and fertility of the other: Obed is born unto Naomi. Beauty and fertility go together in the same woman. To what extent is the *ḥesed* in this case comparable to the one between the two wives of Jacob? Boaz, as we have seen, admits his old age when he compares himself to the young man. His legalistic "trick" consists of extending the levirate to the next generation. Indeed, he is not Ruth's brother-in-law, for he is not Naomi's son, but he may be Naomi's brother-in-law, her husband Elimelech's brother, and then, in marrying Ruth, he marries Naomi a little too, while also identifying with her. For unto her clave Ruth. That is why the neighbors can say: to Naomi a son is born.

Now, there is still the second comparison. It is more complex than it would seem. For there are again two names, this time a male and a female name. The subject to whom Boaz is compared, Parez, is presented as the object of a female subject, Tamar, who bore him unto Judah. The case is highly dubious, and close to illegality, if not illegitimacy, as will become apparent in chapter 4. Parez, in his turn, is like Jacob, the male subject of the first comparison. For they were both born as the "officially" younger one of twins but illegally took the place of the firstborn.

Leah had been veiled in order to gain access to sexuality. Symmetrically, Tamar was forced to veil herself in order to get her due: a child, by the desire of Judah, who, like Boaz, was mistaken about generations. Tamar bore Parez unto Judah, thus correcting the latter's fault. For Judah tried to protect his younger son from the contact with the woman, which he judged lethal, and was thus about to stop the continuity of history. So Tamar corrects a fault committed against woman, for the sake of patrilinear history. While Rachel and Leah corrected the fault of the split between the two aspects of femininity, Tamar corrects a more archaic fault against woman, which is even more destructive: the fault of being afraid of her, and of institutionalizing that fear, that *horror feminitatis*. But there is still Parez. As the son of his mother, he is a transgressor of rules. His name means "break." Breaker of rules, he represents also the "brèche vers une latence" of the cure. Boaz the perfect citizen is compared to him. How can he be compared with the fruit of Tamar's wit and Judah's double standard? Integrating the two laws, Boaz is transgressing as well. In the third chapter, he is still dominated by the sexual standard of Judah and Lot: he is tricked by the woman during his alibi-sleep. This is the third, still more archaic fault committed against woman: the denial of responsibility. He does not yet recognize or acknowledge Ruth, and he is afraid of being confronted by her. He misses the acknowledgment of the woman, like Judah and like Lot, of whom three times it is said that he did not know what he was doing, what happened to him. In chapter 3, Ruth cannot but be the veiled woman, unacknowledgeable, who is denied the status of intersubjective subject by her sexual partner.

As we will see, the success of Tamar's action is precisely there: in the acknowledgment by the father of his own fault. Tamar, said Judah, has been more *just* than he. The comparison, then, raises the problem of the relation between charity and justice, between gift and due. When Boaz goes to court at the city gate, he identifies with Parez the transgressor of rules, son and grandson of Judah, who is like himself a mediator. Boaz becomes the mediator, between generations, sexes, classes, and people, between law and justice, the public and the private, economy and history. Assuming this position as a mediator, participating in collective heroism, Boaz constitutes himself the gate he wished to enter.

The three proper names alluded to in Ruth, and in particular in the court session that gives a statement about the fabula by interpreting it, form a coherent series. Moab, Ruth's country, Lot's son, symbol of fertility as well as of promiscuity, is also the symbol of nonreflective sexuality, where the subject-position is refused, so that no relation between subjects is possible, but only action of a subject on an object. If Ruth deserved the right to be subject to Israelite law, she did so by bridging the gap between nonreflective and self-conscious sexuality. She "turns her neck" to her archaic tribe by correcting its practices. Rachel and Leah manage to go even beyond that: they conquer a whole feminine subjectivity, and Tamar proves that their case is right.

The metatexts that state that Boaz is practicing charity miss the point of the word *ḥesed*, the meaning of which Tamar shows to Judah: justice, rather than charity, due rather than gift. If Boaz is a hero, it is because he dares to assume the point of view of the woman, because he has understood that it is in his interest to do so. He accepts being reflected, by the *mise en abyme*, in a female role. Nonreflective as he was in chapter 3, like Judah and Lot, he becomes shrewd like Tamar in chapter 4. Acknowledging his position of a subject that needs the other to be accomplished as such, he is able to identify with Naomi, she to whom the child is born. Thereby, he earns the place that is reinstated for him in the final genealogy—or is it just the male line that takes over at the end?

The series of transgressing women tells a story by analogy, dispersed among several episodes but still coherent: "the continuity of history, or how to admit love." In other words: the building of the house of Israel, against all odds, against fearful fathers. Together, the three fabulae alluded to become the *mise en abyme* of the history of Israel, paradoxically represented in an antichronological figure that fills in the unavoidable lack of the *present* in any chronology.

Reflecting Reflection

Boaz's awareness of the indispensable part of women in history, and in his own life, which he wishes so badly to insert into history, represents the fruit of reflection as a daring act. It also represents the entrance into the symbolic order that is so full of other subjects. The meaning of the one character that Boaz is could not be understood without the interaction, through the symptoms I have analyzed, with the other characters. That this growing intersubjectivity was signified in the first place by the proper name, seems consistent with the Lacanian account of this passage, which others would perhaps call a rite of passage (Van Gennep 1909). The proper names whose intertextual and intratextual interplay we have been following for a while, end up as partaking in one of the most knotty figures of contemporary narratology, the *mise en abyme*. Why is this little figure of analogy so fascinating, for critics as well as for writers and readers? Its status as troublemaker, as disturber of chronology, as interrupter of the neat linearity of narrative, makes it especially attractive for the purpose of this study. Moreover, it is a privileged concept, in that it has been subject to extensive elaboration in different disciplines: art history, narratology, philosophy (Derrida), semiotics; it has attracted reflection and predilection from writers (Gide, Leiris, Ricardou), and, through the metaphor used to describe it, the mirror, it touches upon Lacanian psychoanalysis.

The mirror has the attraction of a paradox. The notion on which the mirror metaphor is based is that of *reflection*, which is in its turn paradoxical. Language is the source and the means of this paradox. It is anchored in the process of self-identification in which the Lacanian mirror stage is a decisive phase. The dramatic confrontation with the *same* by the perception of the *different* is staged in the *mise en abyme*. The identity is constructed by a dialectic between the unique and the identical. The *mise en abyme*, then, is unique in that it tells metatextually its own version of the fabula, its own story, by repeating the fabula. The figure integrates the mirroring between the imaginary and the symbolic reflection. In the mirror, the subject recognizes itself as a topic, by the mutual focalization of the mirroring and the mirrored subject. In intellectual reflection, the speaking/thinking subject reflects on its own status, thus becoming in its turn an object, radically different.

The most serious flaw of Lucien Dällenbach's important book on the *mise en abyme* is the absence of any reflection on the status of the *mise en abyme* as a sign. However, if it is not a sign, it cannot be, for then it could not function as a reflection. But if it is a sign, it has to be delimited, and there resides the problem, as well as its interest. The problem is, again, two-sided. One of the characteristics of the *mise en abyme* is its virtually endless regressive potential, which so fascinated Leiris in the Dutch cocoa box. This movement destroys any possible linearity of the text. Not only is it impossible to follow the chronology any longer as soon as a *mise en abyme* arises—it arises in order to interrupt it—but also, the limits between the whole and the part, between the text and the metatext, become problematic. For the figure imposes its unique version of the fabula and thus disrupts the version we were reading at the moment it intervened. The status of the detail is thus called into question.

In that respect, the so-called *mise en abyme éclatée*, the fragmented *mise en abyme* that consists of the dispersed elements of a previously assumed *mise en abyme* throughout the whole text, reflects in its turn the effect of *mise en abyme* as a general *mode of reading*. In other words, after the scene of the trial, we will have to turn back, following the etymology of the word "reflection": *to turn our necks* and return to Orpah. We will, then, have to follow the two women once more to the country of Moab, where they will have to return in order to provide us with the elements of reading that the process presupposes. If perfect analogy, reflection, is an illusion, so is chronology.

·4·

ONE WOMAN, MANY MEN, AND THE DIALECTIC OF CHRONOLOGY

The Limits of Higher Criticism

Genesis 38 is a problem for higher criticism. The chapter seems a late insertion, since it has hardly anything to do with the story in which it is inserted, the story of Joseph. Thomas Mann handled the problem in a revealing way when, while writing his voluminous novel *Joseph and His Brothers,* he was confronted with the need for psychological motivation that is required by the novelistic genre. He displaced the episode of Judah and Tamar to the last section of the novel, after the main factors of suspense had been eliminated; that is, after Joseph's misadventures with Potiphar's wife.

There is one major argument supporting the assumption (considered as generally accepted in Speiser 1964) that the Tamar story has been inserted arbitrarily. Not only is there no diegetic link between chapters 37 and 39 on the one hand, and 38 on the other. Not only is there a very slight link in the identity of the characters. More important, there is no chronological continuity between the three chapters.

The unity of the fabula that is thus questioned is, however, a matter of interpretation. The limits of higher criticism lie precisely here. First, one assumes the necessity of unity; then the specific type of unity required is confronted with the text; then and only then the historical status of a text fragment is derived from the result. Preconceptions sometimes precede even the first of these steps. Some scholars, on the other hand, assume that the editorial policy of the authors and editors may have been different from what we are used to; still, they suppose that policy to be stronger or weaker. When they assume it is strong, they will look for traces, symptoms of a specific policy, and, taking it seriously beforehand, they will try to find a motive for the insertion. Unity is in that case as strong a presupposition as in the opposite case. Scholars who start from a specific poetics—their own—will conclude that the text is an arbitrary assemblage of fragments, while others will have the same presupposition of unity but add to that the strong-policy claim.

Scholars of the latter kind, that is, those who assume the editorial policy to have been quite elaborate, have better chances of finding unknown features of biblical poetics. Robert Alter is a case in point (see chapter 5). Confronted with the sequence of Genesis 37–39 and the problem it poses, he argues for a thematic unity as a substitute for the apparent lack of chronological continuity. His interpretation rests on the thematic similarities between the chapters, like the trick, blood, brothers. Although his argument points to the same tension between the two principles as I outlined in the previous chapter, I find Alter's solution unsatisfactory. It is both too easy and too drastic. Chronology is such a central concept, not only to our culture but also to the Bible, that it cannot be disposed of so unproblematically (for repression of time problems, see Fabian 1983). The apparently easy solution entails too drastic an elimination of chronological considerations. The solution remains within the binary opposition between the two narrative devices of chronology and analogy, where I would propose rather to question the concept of chronology as we conceive it in itself. If the previous chapter of this study showed the poetics of metatextuality to be a function of the tension between the two, the following remarks will reinstate chronology with the help of text-internal analogy, starting in Alter's way—that is, thematically—but continuing further analysis within the problematic of the subject. Text-internal analogy is not less metatextual but works on a short-term basis, that is, within the sequence of three following chapters of the same book.

As a case of reception, it is the editorial policy itself that will be used as a starting point. The motivation of the editors who put the three chapters together in this particular order, which apparently is a problem to both philologists and novelists, is in itself an instance of reception. Why did these editors consider these particular elements of folkloric and historical tradition to form a coherent sequence? The question implies the assumption that they did. Let me make my point clear. I do not argue against the results of higher criticism. I do wish to point out some of its presuppositions. But my claim lies elsewhere. The editors have put the three chapters in a sequence. It is their motivation for doing so that I am interested in. Next, once thus edited, the sequence has been preserved with care. This preservation, again, has been motivated, according to the changing interests of the groups that dealt with the sequence. But a first motivation that interrupted all possible others is the acceptance of the sacred character of the text *as edited.* In other words, the decisions, once made, had to be erased, the text's sacredness replacing the human intervention and its motivations. As a result, the authority of the text allowed later readers to lose interest in the unity of the text; since that unity was taken for granted, it ceased being a concern. Hence, it became an ideology (Van Alphen 1986). Now, the first and foremost thematic unity is *love,* especially between 38 and 39. Love, and tricksters. This theme of tricky love is, I want to argue, the immediate symptom of the editorial and of the readerly motivation. But tricksters are narrative agents, and love is a narrative itself.

Then came, in the heyday of the convention of unity, the "higher" critics. Their acceptance of arbitrariness in the process of textual production seems to open up that convention. But in fact, it does not do so. First, the criteria for decisions are in general related to a norm of unity (for an extensive argumentation, see Bal 1988). Second, the assumption of an editorial mistake in the case of Genesis 37–39 rests on an aesthetics of unity whose frustration leads to it. On the other hand, attempts to establish thematic unity as a replacement for narrative chronology apparently accept a different aesthetics (Alter); in fact, they reject the narrative coherence of the sequence on the basis of their own straightforward idea of narrative.

The discussion of unity leads to a dead end because unity is not a textual but a readerly feature, and because it is not a thing but a process. There is as much unity as one looks for, and therein is not the problem. Only if one replaces a concern for unity with a search for motivation does it become possible to see what *happened,* at specific moments, in the process of readerly unification. We can then go back to the chosen starting point, the moment of editorial action, and the assumption that the theme of love and of tricksters motivated it. If that justifies *asking* the question, the answer will only be convincing if it explains not only the presupposed editorial policy but also the subsequent doubts about that policy, that is, the evolution of the ideology of love.

On the Margins of Anachrony:
Paralepsis, or the Deviation from the Straight Path

Formal narratology is opposed to, and struggles against, subjectivity. This polemical attitude motivates the following critique. The study of chronology as a formal structure in narrative fabula-story relations has reached its climax and its limits with Genette's study of Proust (1972; English translation, 1980). Therefore, I will focus on this study as symptomatic of an attempt to void narrative of subjectivity. Rejecting Genette's many categories or ignoring them seems too easy a solution. The problem of the sequence under consideration is too obvious for that. And the relations between the formal approach and the basic subjectivity of all discourse are, as such, relevant issues. *Sidesteps* are an issue in this chapter, both biblical and scholarly, both diegetic and discursive, both moral and narratological ones. Sidesteps are, like *mise en abyme,* a challenge to chronology and, hence, to narrative. Let me start with a sidestep in my own discourse, and discuss Genette's narratological discourse as symptomatic. The relevance of my sidestep will appear shortly. It concerns, of course, the subject in love.

Under the general heading of *anachrony* Genette discusses narrative figures that consist of deviations from the straight path of diegetic chronology. Apparently, subjectivity is a problem that threatens the analysis.

The two basic figures are *analepsis* and *prolepsis,* which Genette rebaptizes because the classical names of retrospection and anticipation "[evoke] the psychological connotations of such terms . . . , which automatically evoke subjective phenomena" (39–40). Depending on possible differences of "reach" and "extent," analepses and prolepses can be internal or external, that is, cover a temporal section situated inside or outside the "principal" fabula. "Reach" is the length of the time stretch they cover, so that they can also stand in a relation of contiguity to the fabula or be cut off from it. There are more distinctions, relevant enough but based on a similar argument and definition.

What interests me here in the first place is the description Genette provides of the different figures of anachrony. Starting from examples by Proust and others, the critic quite soon has recourse to a negative criterion of description: the *ellipsis,* introduced in the paragraph on analepsis and not defined for its own sake. (The omission of a definition can be appreciated for its iconicity; how can the negative be better described?) Ellipsis motivates, occasions, analepsis in that the retrospections are supposedly necessary to fill in previous gaps. Temporal lacunae, the hypothetical ellipses are the occasion of the analepses, since the omission (-lipsis) of the present provokes the adoption (-lepsis) of the past in a later stage. This mode of thought will prove quite to the point for our problematic sequence.

Obviously, and Genette realizes this, the ellipsis in the strict sense can only be manifest in the figures that come to fill it in in the afterthought. How, then, can we delineate the temporal fragments with precision? The problem becomes manifest when Genette continues to discuss the different types of lacunae (in order to keep track of his terminological system, see Table 7).

> But there is another type of gap, of a less strictly temporal kind, created not by the elision of a diachronic section but by the omission of one of the constituent elements of a situation in a period that the narrative does generally cover. An example: the fact of recounting his childhood while systematically concealing the existence of one of the members of his family. . . . Here the narrative does not skip over a moment of time, as in an ellipsis, but it *sidesteps* a given element. This kind of lateral ellipsis . . . we will call a paralipsis. (51–52)

Table 7

	lipsis (omission)		*lepsis (adoption)*	
pro (future)	prolipsis:	future gap	prolepsis:	anticipation
ana (past)	analipsis:	previous gap	analepsis:	retrospection
para (aside)	paralipsis:	concealing information	paralepsis:	extra information

The term "gap," with its complement "less strictly temporal" but situated in a paragraph devoted to the temporal figure *par excellence*, gives insight into the problematic character of Genette's enterprise (for a critique of the term "gap," see Hamon 1984). Is it possible for a phenomenon to be more or less strictly temporal? The concept of temporality presupposes a conceptual articulation of the semantic field; therefore, it owes its existence to a system of thought, not to reality. To establish that conceptual articulation first, and then to anchor certain of its elements in reality, even if stating their problematic nature, is an index of an ontological confusion that questions the foundations of the whole enterprise. However, dealing with ellipsis and its subtype, the paralipsis, in the paragraph on analepsis, Genette is trying to conceive of them in their temporal aspects. The example given points to the same problem, and, as an additional advantage, it holds the same categories as the Genesis sequence. To recount one's childhood is indeed a retrospective act. "Concealing the existence of a member of the family" may be less so: if one conceals, one does so in the act of recounting. To name a member of the family involves, in a way, the restitution of that person in the past. Hence, it is not possible to eliminate the victim of the concealment of that past during which he or she existed on the same premise as his or her luckier relatives. Neither Proust's brother nor Joseph disappears from the hypothetical fabula. In other words: in the past s/he exists, in the present s/he is concealed, and it is precisely because the character is, in the fugitive narrative present, concealed, that he or she is subject to an eventual narrative figure. Yet the criterion, which consists of a definition of narrative fullness through an ideology of the family, needs justification. How can the family be considered as the frame of semiotic fullness while that very fullness is impossible by definition? Paradoxically, the hypothetically concealed brother is concealed because Proust's retrospection cannot possibly reserve a place for him; significantly, the frame is the psychoanalytical nuclear family, which excludes any rival of the same generation, rather than the "real" family. Family against family, present against past, let us still give the other (Genette) or the Other (narratol-

ogy) the benefit of the doubt. The relevance of formalism's sidestep—
and of mine—becomes, it is hoped, clear by now: formalism imposes
forms, structures, whose semantic bases are deeply anchored in a view of
the family. Brothers have, in that structure, a position of analogy to one
another, and a position in the chronology in relation to the father and
the offspring. As we will see, there is no structural place, there, for the
woman who connects the two extremes.

Genette is right, however, when he deals with the figures of paralipsis
within the paragraph on analepsis, and this because of the very negative
character of the figure. The gap cannot be revealed except afterwards,
when, in the future that is the narrative present, the retrospective analepsis comes to fill it in. But that *analepsis-on-paralipsis*, as Genette calls it
with his characteristic sense of humor (53), has a symmetrical counterpart
that is not discussed at the same place. It is the *paralepsis*, which consists
of "taking up . . . and giving information that should be left aside" (195).
This little, marginal figure poses again the problem of the norm in
relation to which it can be defined as a deviation, and there the problem
starts. Genette introduces this figure in the chapter on mood, in the
paragraph on focalization) and not in the chapter on chronology. This
displacement points, again, to a problem of structure. It is another sidestep.

If it is possible to define a temporal figure as analepsis-on-paralipsis,
there is no reason not to include the paralepsis within the analysis of order
and to assume the possibility of the specification *paralepsis-on-analipsis*. It
consists of the presentation of some extra information as an *aside* from the
diegetical chronology, in order to fill in a previous gap. The sidestep is
coming closer now. The status of the figure is even far more convincing
than that of its counterpart. Because the figures of -lepsis are positively
defined, it is clearer in its manifestation, and its analiptical character,
which is its motivation in the theoretically necessary diegetical past, is
often explicitly indicated. Ostensibly absent in Genette's otherwise comprehensive time-system, the paralepsis-on-analipsis is doubly deviant. By
the *asideness* that founds it, it displays the fragility of diegetic coherence
and the unlimited possibilities of transgression. It is easy to imagine a
story where, from paralepsis to paralepsis, chronology disappears in favor of a movement of enlargement; rather than from father to son, the
fabula would develop from brother to brother (as in Genesis 37–38–39),
or sister to cousin, to second cousin, and so forth: what a nightmare!
Many problems of coherence in the Bible can be dealt with in this light.
The subversive character of our little figure is so obvious that the spatial
metaphor on which its concept is based dominates the representation of
the act it constitutes: the deviation from the straight path. If the fabula of
the Bible as a historical book is rigorously chronological, it seems to be in
order to convince us of the very notion that one does not deviate from the

right path at small cost. But at the same time the opposite is shown: one does not stop deviating from the right path; the fabula of the Bible owes its existence to the dialectic of sidesteps, and the fate of humanity has been represented by spatial deviation rather than by the unavoidable progression of time that is its consequence: the forcible departure from paradise lost.

Tamar from Father to Son, or On Subversion

Let me summarize the problem. If we consider only classical structuralist categories such as events, the structure of the fabula, chronology, space, and the identity of the actantial subject, the biblical tale of Tamar and Judah (Genesis 38) is a deviation; it is indeed a detour between 37 (the sale of Joseph by his brothers) and 39 (Joseph's misadventures with Potiphar's wife). What is the function, between those two stories of Joseph's bad luck, of the short episode on Tamar, Judah's daughter-in-law, or, from another angle, of the story of Judah, Joseph's brother? There, rather than concealing a member of the family—as Genette accused Proust of doing—the text adds a brother, and that to a story that could very well do without the unworthy brothers who have just eliminated themselves in their attempt to eliminate the chosen. As a clear case of paralepsis, the episode is rather obviously misplaced. Too obviously so. This position of the tale mirrors the fabula itself: at Timnath, Judah deviated from the right path for the purpose of whoring. On the axis of selection, of analogy, of metaphor, however, there is evidence of the opposite view. Semantic similarities and dissimilarities, shifts and displacements, which all have to do with family relationships, provide more than enough reasons for considering the juxtaposition of these three chapters in the final version of the book of Genesis as a well-founded, significant sequence. Analogy provides the key to the interpretation of a specific, dialectic view of chronology. Similarities are censored by displacements, and this very process reveals the hidden causality of the juxtaposition. In all three chapters, deceit is committed with the help of an object used as a pledge or as proof, each time a significant part of the victim's outfit. In 37, the victim's brothers are the deceivers, in 39, it is a woman. In 38, the deceiver is also a woman, but she seems justified in her reaction to the injustices done to her. In 38, both a woman and brothers are involved. Thus ends our first survey of analogy. The analogies concern love, relations between generations and sexes, and danger. Since only in chapter 38 is there a lethal woman, this middle episode may be assumed to mediate between the two others. But to our relief, she also restores life, while the man in that story is both a trickster and a near-killer. Hence, things are not so simple. The chronology of the three chapters is not as easily reconstituted

as narratology would like. Judah still lives with his father when his younger brother is sold; hence, from that point of view, there is little reason to
presuppose an underlying analipsis. Chapter 38 would then be a pure
paralepsis without any inkling of analysis. On the other hand, it is impossible to presuppose a parallel prolipsis that would explain the sequence:
38 would then presumably fill in a chronological gap between 37 and 39.
First, and the argument is decisive, the prolipsis is a contradiction in
terms: the absurdity consists of claiming a future omission, filled in beforehand. The chronology of reading does not allow such a claim. The
second reason is diegetical. As the stretch of time between the selling of
Joseph by his brothers and his unsuccessful defloration in Egypt is not
specified, there are as many arguments for as against the hypothesis of a
"prolipsis." On the one hand, Joseph must have gone through many
phases before he came into the position he occupies in Potiphar's house,
and that position is the *sine qua non* of the adventure. He had made a long
trip, and he began his career on the lowest rung, as a foreign slave. On the
other hand, the adventure itself contradicts the hypothesis of a long lapse
of time; his defloration is still not realized, and, moreover, his later
confrontation with his brothers shows that they are still under the authority of the father, while in 38 Judah is already a mighty patriarch.

Starting with the plausibility of analipsis, chapter 38 outgrows the
frame which thus seems to include it. This structure is not without meaning. On the contrary, it is an iconic sign as complex as its temporal
structure suggests it to be. Also, it is a challenge to the very narratological
concept that is meant to describe it. As a paralepsis, it signifies from the
beginning Judah's deviation from the right path at Timnath, the very
site where Samson committed the same transgression, though without
going as far as paralepsis. The deviation from the path is itself a sign of
the deviation that Judah, already guilty of *selling* his brother, is going to
endorse: the *buying* of his daughter-in-law. We will have to follow this
specialist in family business.

It is possible right now to consider the displacement of the chapter not
as an editorial mistake but as a significant act, motivated and related to
the endorsement of paralepsis as sign. We may assume a case of lapsus, a
slip, of the intervention of the unconscious, which, far from eliminating
the episode for the sake of clarity, has dictated its position at this place
for reasons we will have to clarify.

Juxtaposition, or Similarity behind Displacement

If it is problematic, even impossible, to specify to what extent the paralepsis that constitutes chapter 38 is based on an analipsis or on a pro-

lipsis, we can definitely say that it does disturb chronology. Hence is established a competition between the eminently narrative chronology and the paraleptical juxtaposition that cannot but be founded in the analogy of a spatial metaphor. I will assume for the moment that the displacement that led critics to propose the removal of the chapter from its context, without finding a more suitable place for it, is a form of Freudian censorship; in order to neutralize it, a first move should consist of stressing the relations between the three chapters that constitute the problematic sequence. Only after highlighting the spatial metaphor can we, in a second phase, discover the hidden causality that is the site of a different, otherwise strong, chronology.

As has been said already, family relations are thematized in the three chapters. Each time, someone is deceived with the help of an object. In 37, father Jacob is deceived by his sons with the help of Joseph's colorful cloak, soaked in blood that is not his. In 38, Judah deceives Tamar, promising his youngest son without intending to execute the promise. There is no object involved here. But in the same chapter, Tamar deceives Judah, covering her face with a veil and using the patriarchal attributes not as payment but as evidence of Judah's responsibility. In 39, Joseph's cloak is again used, this time by Potiphar's wife, in order to deceive her husband about the identity of the subject of seduction. In each case, the metonymic bond is not strong enough: the object is a part of the subject's equipment, not of himself; it is a metonymy but not a synecdoche. Thus it leaves room for *méconnaissance* or falsification. The object is, however, not just any part of the victim's outfit but a significant or central part, and, therefore, it is logical that it is taken as evidence of his identity and hence as synecdochic. Since the object is acknowledged at the end as absolute evidence, it becomes a metaphor for the subject, who can, with the help of that reification, recover his subjective status that was in danger. This complex play with semiosis ("used in order to lie," Eco 1976:11) is part of a fundamental questioning of the subject.

As we have seen already, in the Christian reception of biblical tales, a moralistic attitude is often predominant. The tales are considered as incomplete parables where the moral point has to be discovered by the recipients. The case of Samson showed how easily the moral guilt is attributed to the woman. If we take this characteristic of biblical reception into account, the omission of Gen. 38 in children's Bibles and the accusations of Tamar in popular commentaries point in the same direction. The problem raised by the juxtaposition of these three tales makes, however, for the censorship in children's Bibles. Similarities and differences between the tales make the guilt question in 38 problematic. Within the communication process of the Bible, this uncertainty functions as a provocation. Modern readers feel uncomfortable with unclear moral values of this sort and try to escape them by disambiguating the tale. In my analysis of the tale I will argue that this need for moral certainty is related to a psychological problem, raised in the three stories and handled by the edition. This problem could very well be the profound reason for the location of 38, but not without another displacement.

In 37, the brothers ill-use their innocent younger brother. In 39, the woman misuses the same innocent young man. In 37, he suffers for his filial obedience. Separated from his father, facing woman in 39, he keeps his innocence, which now becomes sexual purity. In 37 and in 38, the father is deceived. In 38, however, the father is also a deceiver. In both cases, the father protects his young son. In 39, the father is replaced by the social father-figure, the boss. This father is deceived like the father in 37 and in 38, but he participates in the misuse of the son by letting himself be deceived. He thus resembles both the father in 37, who cannot further protect the son, and the father in 38, who deceives in his turn, even if, this time, he is unaware of it.

Two more displacements among the three tales censor the analogies. The object with the help of which the deception takes place consists of clothes in 37 and 39. Undressing the innocent victim is obviously the first step toward deception and ill-treatment. In 38, the object is threefold and consists of the signs of paternal dignity. With the father being the deceived person, undressing hardly seems appropriate, but the attributes belonging to his social position are taken away from him. Second, the place of sexuality is different in each case. In 37, the whole topic seems irrelevant, except for three "details": the undressing, the blood smeared onto the dress, and the separation from the family, which puts the young man in sexual danger—see 39. In 39, sexuality moves from the margins to the center. The undressing here has a literally sexual purpose: the dress is considered as proof of sexual misbehavior, and the still innocent young man is imprisoned for having undressed—officially for having committed, but in fact for having refused, the sexual act. The place of the brothers moves in the opposite direction. In 37, they are central and clearly guilty, as is the woman in 39. In 38, they are less central, not involved in the deception (except for the youngest brother, who is indirectly involved), and their position in sexual matters is highly problematic. In 39, they have disappeared.

The dialectic of analogies and displacements, of repression and the return of the repressed, enhances a problematization of the subject of which I will sketch the outlines below. The question of the subject will be considered as an index of a problem emblematized by this text, which can be summarized as the confrontation of the subject with its own chronology.

Onan's Offspring, or How to Conceive Safely

The problem of chronology is, as we have seen, closely related to the question of the subject. The first problem in this chapter concerns the position of the son as a narrative subject. In 37, Joseph, the future hero of chastity, is denied any subject position. He does not speak, but he is spoken about, decided upon. He does not act but is acted upon. Sent by his father, he is taken over by his elder brothers, who dispose of him by making him an absolute object: a slave. In 39, he has recovered some of his narrative powers, though he remains in a filial position: he speaks, teaching his tormentor how well he observes his filial duties by leaving to the father what belongs to the father. Eventually he focalizes, noticing the dangers in the empty house (11). He acts, by fleeing, by refusing to sleep with his boss's wife. The activities remain minimal and negative. Joseph's powers are reduced to the possiblity of avoidance: to refuse, to flee from the woman, to avoid dangers. In spite of this slight progress, he is still victimized, objectified; he is spoken of but calumniated, focalized but misjudged, acted upon but misused.

In 38, there are three sons—the magic number of completeness, the exhaustion of all possibilities. The first son is killed, by God, for unspecified reasons. The boy died when he was to marry Tamar. Was the marriage consummated? Tamar has not yet conceived. The law of levirate provides for her. She has the right to be given to the next brother, a "right" bestowed on the woman, as we have seen, when she becomes a childless widow. One goal is obviously to provide an offspring for the husband's family. Er, the first son, does not accede to the position of a narrative subject. He is given a wife by one father and is killed by the other father, probably before he can act upon her. He is as powerless as the Joseph of 37. Onan, the next son, is better off. He at least is addressed. He is entitled to focalization and action. What he focalizes is, however, his own secondary position, the derivative nature of his eventual action. What he then acts out is refusal, a symmetrical counterpart to Uriah's refusal: like the Joseph of 39, he refuses to have sex with the woman who is imposed on him. His explicit motive is jealousy. Paradoxically, he envies his brother who died without conceiving.

According to Speiser (1964), the name *Er* means *vigilant* and the name *Onan* means *deceit*. Whether or not these etymologies can be taken seriously, what is Onan's lie? Perhaps the alleged motive of his jealousy: he may be envious not of the offspring his seed is to provide for his brother, but of Er's vigilance. At any rate, there is deceit in the reception of this episode. For Onan gave his name to onanism, while his sin is not masturbation but *coitus interruptus*. The omission, in this displacement, is the presence of the woman. Judah, of all people, interprets Onan's and Er's deaths as due to similar causes. In verse 11 he sends Tamar away, for fear that his youngest son might also die from the contact with her. He promises to have her marry him later, thus assuming that the other two boys were too young for marriage; this prematurity caused love to be lethal. In doing this, he protects his younger son against the danger of the premature contact with the lethal woman. Judah's attitude makes the interpretation of Onan's sin more than plausible, and the repression of the woman's share in the reception all the more significant.

This account of the three brothers' subject positions suggests that they represent three phases in the maturation process of the young male. So far, the process ends negatively; Er was a weak subject like the Joseph of 37, Onan is slightly stronger, but capable only of negative action, while Shelah is simply replaced. In Bremond's terms (1972), we can label this sequence an incomplete narrative cycle. A complete cycle opens upon a situation, a program or process of amelioration or deterioration, and ends with a result. Here, the programmed development fails. The failure represents an ideological position. Judah's goal was an impossible one: to have offspring and to keep his sons in safety. As he states it himself in verse 11, these two goals are incompatible, for marriage would kill his son, while without marriage the seed would be spilled, and the family would die out. Judah finds a way out of this dilemma: he replaces the son.

Between 37 and 39, this replacement is regressive. Jacob, in 37, could not protect his son any further; he had to let him go and be delivered to the danger represented by the woman in 39. Judah protects his son, but he does so making him powerless, as powerless as his dead brothers. Judah succeeds where Jacob seemed to fail: he keeps his son, and doubly conceives. But this victory of the father over the son is an ad hoc solution, for it contravenes the structure of history, in which generations must replace each other progressively. According to the lesson that Genesis 3 taught us, birth and death presuppose each other; together, they make history.

Tamar's Matchmaking: The Mirror Stage

In comparison with the image of Jacob as a weakling, which he displays several times, and with the tendency of his sons to take over his paternal power, as they do not only in 37 but also in the case of their sister Dinah's rape (Genesis 34), Judah seems more valiant and efficient than his father, Jacob. In fact, he overdoes it. He manages to protect his son, but he denies him access to the adult world. His protection is domination, his replacement, castration. Jacob, when he thinks his son is dead, will not let his other children comfort him. Judah, after losing two sons and a wife, is ready to be comforted. His rebellion against the course of history and against the laws of narrative, then, comes to stand in another light. It looks more and more like unreflected stubbornness and, indeed, his subsequent behavior displays the same features.

The confrontation between Judah and Tamar in 14–26 is a confrontation of two relatively strong subjects, each displaying a specific competence. Judah is powerful whereas Tamar is smart. The sequence is often presented as an example of optimism with respect to the position of women in the Bible. Indeed, Tamar's victory, due only to her wit, sets the limits to patriarchal power. On closer inspection, however, her subject position, strong as it is, turns out to be limited in its turn by its being framed between the death of the weak sons and the birth of the successors to the father. More than an easy moral victory, as most readings suggest, the tale represents a struggle, not yet won, not yet accomplished, but significant in that it demonstrates the dependency of each subject on the other. The male subject, split into the fearful sons and the powerful father, is incapable of assuming his sexuality, while the female subject, strong because of her attraction and fertility, is denied power.

The confrontation is divided into two phases. In 14–19, Tamar acts, disguised as a whore. At least, that is how Judah interprets her veiled apparition; in fact, the word used to describe her (*qedēšâ*, ritual prostitute) is different from the word Judah uses (*zônâ*, whore) and means something like sacred: holy and cursed. In fact, the traditional translation, "cult prostitute," is thoroughly inappropriate. The custom is a socially accepted one, and, although sexuality is involved, it is not commercial.

The difference between whore and ritual "prostitute" is crucial and sheds some light on the nature of the injustice done to Tamar. If the whore is despised because she is overly sexual, the ritual "prostitute" is respected. Devoted to the fertility goddess, her role is probably to help men overcome their fear of defloration. This disguise completes Tamar's position as a woman. She starts as a virgin, becomes, but ambiguously, a wife, only to be widowed immediately; she then acts as a ritual "prostitute" and is considered a whore—a significant error—and ends up as a mother without a husband. Her sexuality is clearly rendered problematic by the men in her life. The wife widowed, the cult "prostitute" made whore, the mother "not known" anymore: these transformations all point to the taboo of virginity, so well described by Freud (1918), and the subsequent taboo of sex with a respectable woman, to which Freud devoted another essay (1912).

She seduces Judah into giving her his paternal attributes as a pledge for the kid (a traditional ritual sacrifice) he has promised. This passage is the only one in which Judah is not in command. His desire makes him dependent on Tamar. She is the subject of speech, of focalization (she rightly analyzes the situation), and of action, stating the conditions of the transaction in which her womb is at stake. Her victory is, however, only partial, as will become apparent shortly. The second phase, 24–26, confronts Judah with the consequences of Tamar's wit and his own double standards. Here, Judah is again in command, is ready to misuse his power and condemn to death the woman *guilty of his own act.* He is merging the subjects. But the other subject intervenes, showing him what he is doing. She wins: Judah looks into the mirror she holds up to him and he admits his fault. Thus she saves him from the danger of endorsing himself the contempt he holds against the whore/ritual "prostitute." From then on, Judah respects her. And she bears him two sons. The course of history, interrupted by Tamar's childless state, is resumed, as is the course of the story of Joseph.

What exactly is Tamar's role? She is a focalizer in the first place. She sees what Judah does not see. In 14, she sees the injustice done to her. In 16–17, she sees that Judah is not to be trusted. Judah, in his turn, sees a whore instead of a relative. In 25, she forces him to see the truth. In fact, her wit, used to restore what was wrong, serves to make Judah see his own (neurotic) errors. His error was the illusion that the course of history could continue while he protected the son from women. Instead, the historical chronology has to be restored: man has first to do away with his fear of woman and then the new generation can be conceived. To show him this, Tamar has to veil herself, seeing without being seen. The double camouflage is needed; the man is so scared that the woman has to cover herself in order to trick him into having sex; and because the truth to be revealed, his own fear, is so shameful, it can only be uncovered under cover of a stratagem. "Discern," Tamar says to Judah in 25, "whose these are." *Discernment* is what she teaches him. Her action does not provide her with the husband that was her goal. But it does provide Judah with the offspring he was longing for. As in many biblical tales, the woman is used for her indispensable share in the course of history, as the sidestep that restores broken chronology. As is often the case, she is also used to teach man insight into his own paralyzing neuroses. Delilah has the same function toward Samson. Tamar's role, too, is that of the psychoanalyst: in dialogue, the subject is forced to look into the mirror and witness his own subjective weakness. Overprotective fathers paralyze their sons and thus, by trying to remain the only subject, kill their own family and stop history.

Genesis 38, then, remains ambiguous, as far as the guilt of deception is concerned. But the deeper issue at stake is not that question of guilt. As an account of insight into self won by the help of the feared woman, the tale serves as a warning not to fear for Joseph too much. The very dangers he is entangled in by his contact with woman will prove to be the source of his future power. In fact, that is what happens: from the prison, he will be called to reign.

The weak position of Judah's sons is reflected in his own weakness: the powerful father is helpless without the other. He is dependent, as we all are, on the place he occupies in the system, the Other. Narration is an expression of the system. The history of the formation of the subject is interrupted here only to show how unavoidable the course of chronology is. The paralepsis, then, does not in the first place signify Judah's deviation, even if that sidestep is obviously part of the demonstration; it is in the first place a sign of its own impossibility. Just like anachrony in general, this subversive little figure, dependent as it is on the subject, cannot, by itself, interrupt chronology. At most, it can hold up a mirror to the story. In that mirror, the image is analogical within a specific chronology: what seemed to come first changes places; what seemed certain becomes problematic. And that precisely is the function of subversion.

·5·

SEXUALITY, SIN, AND SORROW: THE EMERGENCE OF THE FEMALE CHARACTER

Characterizing Character

It is obviously not arbitrary that this book ends with the beginning. The first love story of the Bible, the first love story of our culture, is the one that has been most generally abused, presented as evidence that it was the woman who began it all, that hers is all the guilt; in short, the story is widely adduced as a justification for misogyny. It has not always been used in that way, however. Angenot (1980), for example, shows how in seventeenth-century France, Eve was often praised in unexpected ways. Eve's position as supermother, competing with Mary in that function, excludes unambiguous judgment, and there the problem starts. Christian morality has to carry such a painful burden of ambivalence, of admiration *and* contempt, that its mythical motivations cannot be monolithic. After the preceding analyses, in which a particular feature of the narrative subject was the focus, this last chapter will combine several features in order to shed more light on the relations between modern views of narrative art and ideological evolution. Character will be considered a concept so central to narrative that in it the other aspects of subjectivity combine. In this chapter, the question of the problematic status of the concept itself in literary theory and poetics will be considered as symptomatic and will serve as a starting point for a questioning of its self-evidence. Analogy and chronology are involved again, but this time chronology will be considered from a different, that is, a non-diegetical, point of view.

As an example of reception, early Christian reaction to the story will be discussed. In spite of its exaggerated misogyny, "Paul's" view of women, as it is expressed in a well-known passage (1 Tim. 2:11–14), is not basically different from, say, common Christian morality. The fragment chosen makes such a clear case that it seemed appropriate to me to end this book with a direct confrontation of Jewish myth and Christian ideology. In the course of the long history of Western criticism and poetics, characters have never been described in a satisfactory way theoretically. On the other hand, character is a major concern of what is called "practical criticism"; both the term and the enterprise are dubious, among other reasons because they presuppose an opposition between theory and practice that has doubtlessly impeded the elaboration of a theory of character, a practice I will avoid here. The relevance of the category of character for a comprehensive theory of narrative is obvious. Nevertheless, most attempts fail to construct it, at least partially, and this may be due to several reasons, which I will not seek to analyze. But one of them has to be singled out here. Theories are presented in order to arrive at the definition, explanation, classification, and evaluation of characters, but without a clear demarcation between those different aims. Terms applied to characters with the purpose of generalizing about them are, for instance, the following:

(a) *descriptive terms:* confrontation; transgression of boundaries; differentiation; subject of action; bundles of features
(b) *normative terms:* completeness; freedom; individuality; development; complexity; depth; penetration into the "inner life"; representation of general human values
(c) *explanatory and descriptive terms:* projection of human conflicts
(d) *definitional terms:* proper(ly) name(d)

The first group (a) can possibly be considered as descriptive, though the first two features have a normative connotation. They are not exclusive, however; their range goes far beyond character alone. The next group (b) consists of terms that are both normative and classificatory. In spite of the fact that these terms are seldom claimed to be definitional, figures in a text are often said not to be "real characters" because they do not meet these standards. The psychoanalytical idea of projection (c) is both explanatory and descriptive; it concerns character less than the structure provided by characters and action. Finally, proper name (d) is a sufficient but not necessary condition; hence, it is not a condition at all but only a possible label. It is both too thin as a definition and tautological. Nevertheless, it is a useful starting point for a discussion, which will be given below.

I do not want to claim that this confusion needs to be unraveled in order to arrive at a correct theory of character. Its persistence, though, should be explained. Attempts to overcome it have been made, recently, by Hamon (1983) and Rimmon-Kenan (1983). Hamon opts for a strict limitation of the concept of character to a few semiotic categories ("bundles of features"); Rimmon-Kenan, on the contrary, attempts to accommodate most aspects in a coherent set of concepts and distinctions. Significantly, Hamon thoroughly studies a limited corpus of realist texts in depth, while Rimmon-Kenan claims general validity. Both works are valuable and helpful for the further study of narrative. Neither accounts for the ideological effect of characters and for the concept of humanity that sustains them. In my view, that effect is a highly relevant issue in a socially oriented poetics.

Indeed, the concept of character is itself increasingly denounced as an ideologically suspect category. Many discussions on the status of character in modern literature claim it to be a strategy of bourgeois literature, used for the purpose of naturalizing bourgeois ideology as self-evident and true. It is in these discussions that the notion of the proper name comes up. This emphasis is understandable. As the fixed point to which the illusion of wholeness can attach itself, the proper name is the shortest and the most definite sign of a character. It is its textual marker, embodying its stability and its continuity. But in modern fiction and criticism it is the very stability of characters, as a paradigm of the stability of the sign in general, that is questioned. Changing proper names (Robbe-Grillet), abbreviating or, on the contrary, excessively semanticizing them (Duras), or rejecting them altogether (Sarraute) seems to constitute an efficient attack on the concept of character and the realism it is claimed to presuppose.

"The proper name is a sufficient (but not necessary) pre-condition of creating a character," writes Weinsheimer (1979) in his plea for a semiotic criticism of character, and he goes on to describe the lack of continuity of the name in Austen's *Emma* as evidence for the necessity of the type of criticism he is advocating. Roland Barthes, on the other hand, sees the impossibility of writing the proper name, taken as a synonym of character, as a characteristic of modern literature: "What is obsolescent in today's novel is not the novelistic, it is the character; what can no longer be written is the Proper Name" (1974:95). Nathalie Sarraute (1965:84) advocates the description not of characters but of an anonymous, prehuman stratum as a replacement of realistic *personae*. In all these cases, the proper name is seen as the most embarrassing aspect of character, as the thing that determines its suspect stability. With a striking historical naïveté, the tendency toward undifferentiation of characters in modern literature presents itself as a reaction against nineteenth-century realism, in which a bourgeois individualistic ideology is denounced (Ricardou 1971, is the most obvious example). The eighteenth-century anti-novel is mostly ignored, as is medieval allegory, where proper names and common nouns are conflated.

This stream of "anti-character" literature both precedes and is contemporary with the school of poetics that failed spectacularly in its attempts to integrate the concept of character into its too exclusively action-oriented models: structuralism. The already mentioned opposition to the ideology of realism is offered as an honorable excuse for this failure.

Rimmon-Kenan (1983) refutes the idea that the failure of a theory of character is due mainly to an ideological stance. Without denying the importance of that aspect, she conceives the failure, rather, as the result of basic problems inherent in the concept itself. Two of these problems are the mode of existence ("people or words") and its relation to the fabula ("being or doing"). For both problems, Rimmon-Kenan proposes a solution in the form of a compromise. Her solution to the latter problem goes in the direction of reversible and relative interdependence. Depending on the goal of reader or critic, each aspect can be stressed as determining the other. Action leads to a concept of being, while being predicts a certain type of action. In most narratives, features and actions mutually restrict each other's possibilities.

The proper name, or some other sign that posits the textual existence of a character, on the one hand, and a subject position in relation to action on the other, may then be considered as the minimal requirements for the construction of a character. The project is completed by the attribution of features by direct or indirect characterization. Direct characterization posits the priority of being, while indirect characterization favors the priority of action.

Two problems are inherent in this, or any, definition of character. First, it neglects semiotic chronology. I do not mean the linear unfolding of the fabula, which was discussed in chapter 4, or the development of the character in the course of the story; within such a definition, it is possible to accommodate the development of characters. But the existence of characters in a stable and unchanging, if fictive, ontology is part of the very assumption that they change. In this view, they exist from the first time they are mentioned until the end. It is only that we don't know everything about them. The story progressively reveals the missing information so that we can add, reject, or change features in order to complete the image. We do not question their continuous existence as the being we come to know at the end.

Semiotic chronology is involved, however, when we conceive of characters as a product of a textual development that constructs them, piece after piece, by the signs; characters, then, "exist" only insofar as they have been signified. This process results in different types of character constructions. "Emma Woodhouse," for example, does exist as the signified of this proper name from the beginning of the novel, since the name appears right away, while "Eve" exists only at the end of Genesis 3, where her name is mentioned for the first time. What existed before was an earth creature, then a woman, next an actant, then a mother, and, finally, a being named "Eve." While the development of "Emma" displays a continuous changing of a full being, that of this character in Genesis displays a slow construction out of the continuous restriction of possibilities. This chronology is not that of the fabula, in which characters develop just as people do in real life, from infancy to adulthood or from innocence to insight, but that of the semiotic construction of their concept. In this chronology, the proper name has an important function: it provides the illusion of fullness.

Second, such a definition of character tries to grasp it as a single category. Stress on the interdependence of being and action, for example, obliterates the fact that the character stands in a similar relation of interdependence with other characters, other textual elements, or higher levels of abstraction. Exclusive focus on the relation between character and action misses the point of the relation between character as a particularization and type as a generalization. This relation is one of the important textual sites of ideology. It also misses the formation of characters and their features by opposition and analogy. As we have seen, analogy stands in tension with chronology: it establishes stability, while chronology constantly points to the differences between the respective phases of its development. By an unavoidable spatial metaphor, then, analogy can be considered as the lateral counterpart to chronology, its paralepsis.

In proper names, both of the weaknesses of the traditional approaches to character meet. The name's central place stimulates an ideologically biased reading strategy that I will call the *retrospective fallacy*. It consists of the projection of an accomplished and singular named character onto previous textual elements that lead to the construction of that character. It is this circularity that enhances the realistic illusion (cf. Brooks 1984). It is my contention that this fallacy contributes to the production of those narrativizations of ideologies which we call myths.

In order to demonstrate these points, I will follow the construction of character in what is often assumed to be the account of the first pair of characters of our literature: the two creation stories of Genesis 1 and 2. This is obviously not a random choice, and it is subject to the suspicion of analogical reasoning. However, I will argue the contrary: the strong analogy between fabula (which represents the creation of humanity) and story (which constitutes the construction of character) has been so little taken into account by readers that its mode and relevance are clearly not self-evident. Moreover, the type of story that is not read for suspense because its outcome is already known stimulates the repression of the tension between chronology and analogy, hence the narrative nature of the stories.

In my attempt to separate the extant myth of "Eve" from the myth of creation as it is recorded in Gen. 1–3, I will insist on the linearity of reading. I do not claim that this is a "better" or "more natural" reading strategy, only that it is a possible one. This possibility already undercuts the exclusiveness of the other reading, i.e., the paradigmatic one. I will demonstrate the difference between the two myths in order to show the functioning of the retrospective fallacy as a major factor in the production of the sexist myth of "Eve," the derivation of which from this text is far from inevitable.

The Emergence of a Myth: Collocation

"Let the woman learn in silence with all subjection. But I suffer not a woman to teach, nor to usurp authority over the man, but to be in silence. For Adam was first formed, then Eve. And Adam was not deceived, but the woman being deceived was in the transgression" (1 Tim. 2:11–14). This passage, from the letter to Timothy, presents two of the eleven principal arguments for misogyny cited by Trible (1978:73) as having their basis in the second creation story and the story of the fall, Gen. 2:4b–3:27. More recently, Alter (1981:146) sums up the common interpretation of the text as follows: "[it is] an etiological tale intended to account for the existence of woman, for her subordinate status, and for the attraction she perennially exerts over man." Most of the arguments collected by Trible cannot in fact be derived from the biblical text at all, and she convincingly refutes them. The relevant passages that I shall be examining in this chapter are those concerning the creation of the female body, the transgression, and its consequences.

As for "Paul's" arguments specifically, they are both the most frequently brought forward and the most obviously wrong. They are so in three senses. As factual reports of the story, they do not find support in the text when it is carefully read; even if they were to do so, the proper conclusion from these (fictive) facts would not necessarily be these value judgments; and, even if those judgments were justified, there would not be the slightest logical link between them and the prohibition based on them. As I will argue later, it is not obvious that Adam, the man, was first formed; even if he had been, that gives him no superiority in quality—on the contrary; even if he were better made, there is hardly any necessary relation between, on the one hand, being a less successful product of divine pottery and, on the other, one's ability to talk, teach, and to exercise authority. As for the deception, neither of the two human beings was deceived, and both transgressed equally.

My point in this chapter is no more than it was in the preceding ones to establish anachronistically a "feminist" content of the story. It is now time to eliminate explicitly this possible misunderstanding by making my position clear. Certainly, the celebration of woman as the ancient earth- or mother-goddess of which Eve is sometimes claimed to be a leftover (Phillips 1984) may be partly found in the mythical text of Genesis, whose origin is not necessarily coherent. On the other hand, as in the other love stories, the mainstream of biblical ideology is obviously patriarchal. Instead of opting for either a feminist or a sexist reading, both equally false, I have already suggested that there are traces of a *problematization* of man's priority and domination. This holds for most of the Bible, and Genesis is no exception.

The reason for this situation is obvious. The burden of domination is hard to bear. Dominators have, first, to establish their position, then to safeguard it. Subsequently, they must make both the dominated *and* themselves believe in it. Insecurity is not a prerogative exclusively of the dominated. The establishing of a justifying "myth of origin," which has to be sufficiently credible and realistic to account for common experience, is not that simple a performance. Traces of the painful process of gaining control can therefore be perceived in those very myths. They serve to limit repression to acceptable, viable proportions.

As for the present case, these considerations entail the following points. If my interpretation of Eve's position shows her in a more favorable light than do the common uses of the text, I do not want to suggest that this is a feminist, feminine, or female-oriented text. Rather, I will try to account for the nature and function of a patriarchal myth that is related to an ideology that cannot be monolithic. Efforts to make it so are the more desperate, since theirs is an impossible aim. The traces of problematization of the represented ideology do not therefore automatically lead to any improvement of the situation.

But, as I said, this is not my main point. Nor is it my first goal here to denounce the uses that have been made of the text, though that is certainly a more interesting issue. For the confrontation between, on the one hand, the extant mythical text and the documents of its later use, like "Paul's" version, and the subsequent innumerable texts that produce the myth as it still functions, displays a chronological evolution of patriarchy that holds a paradox.

Since it is obvious that ancient Hebrew society, as well as most of its contemporary societies, was thoroughly misogynist—for anyone to whom this is not self-evident, the books of Laws provide useful reading in their evident contempt for the female body—and since, on the other hand, today's Western society claims to have evolved toward respect for equal rights and emancipation, we could expect an evolution from a sexist text to more "equal" readings. We could expect commentators, for example, to stress the positive sides of the Eve character and the negative ones in

Adam, both readings being possible, so that a more equal image of the first human couple might emerge, especially when moral consequences are drawn from it. The fact that the opposite is the case, as I have already demonstrated for the Samson and Delilah story, provides insight into the dynamic nature of myth, into the current state of sexual ideology, and into the necessity of *reversal* as a political move (Derrida 1972: 56–57). Nevertheless, it does seem rather discouraging that we have to appeal to ancient Jewish Patriarchs to defend our character against today's progressive atheists.

In the context of this study, the most interesting point in "Paul's" words—and my motive for taking the quotation as a starting point— seems to me to be the "collocation" of the emergence of the female body in narrative signs and the assumption of the moral corruption of the character endowed with that body. As I will demonstrate, the proper name is the *site* of this collocation. If "Paul" uses this self-evident combination as an argument for the elimination of women from the realm of moral and intellectual authority, it serves equally well for the justification of pornography, rape, and other semiotic and physical kinds of violence. *Mens insana in corpore insano*: since both sides of the character are considered as irredeemably inferior, and this in the context of an uncanny conflation of both, misuse operates against both sides, spirit ("Paul") and body (rapists and pornographers).

Of course, it has been a common insight since the popularization of Freudianism that the female body scares man by its otherness, its "lack" and its obscurity; that, on the other hand, the boy's discovery that the idealized and monopolized mother is a sexual entity, and hence publicly available, inspires the little future patriarch with contempt for her as a moral being. Both reflexes have their causes, their contemporary origins, their projectional and self-destructive aspects. (For a wonderfully illuminating account of the consequences of these reflexes, see Keller 1983). But this does not necessarily entail an automatic *collocation*, the saying-together, the absolutely unavoidable urge to take for granted that *since* Eve's body is claimed to be a lesser performance than Adam's, she is morally the weaker one, available for—or, by another projectional move, embodying—the forces of corruption: a combination of concepts so automatic that it becomes *the* semiotization of the female.

This collocation has a narratological and an anthropological impact. From a narratological point of view, I claim that the development from one myth—the text as it stands—into the other—the sexist view spelled out by "Paul"—is the result of the retrospective fallacy. For example, one set of readers of Genesis 1–3, namely the historical-critical school, interpreting the combination of two creation stories and the story of the fall, has projected the last part of the third story onto the second, repressing the first and considering it as an alien, later account. They have read in this manner because they have failed to understand that this text is a semiotic object. As such, it creates not the world, but narrative. It presents an account of the making of humanity within a progressive development of character. Missing that point, then, results in assuming the retrospective fallacy: readers project the accomplished characters Adam and Eve, who appear at the very end of the third story, onto their previous stages of particularization. Hence, the concept of character is at once a cause of the sexist myth and a means by which to deconstruct it.

From an anthropological point of view, it is my contention that this collocation is another instance of an ambivalent conceptual "origin" that had to be repressed after being mythified: the split of body and soul, an alien invention, which, just like the patriarchy, became such a heavy burden on the shoulders of the same humanity that invented it. Man, dissatisfied with himself, frightened of his drives and disgusted by his demanding body, found a way out by assuming that this body was very different from himself. But he knew very well that this would not work. The power of the body just would not make sense in such a structure. Therefore the perception, external and hence monolithic, of the woman who in her otherness could seem more whole, posed a problem of envy. Envying her apparent wholeness, blaming her otherness, he decided she was entirely corrupt. Thus, the myth of origin was corrupted. The split between body and soul was retrospectively projected upon Eve as character as it became available after the working of the retrospective fallacy: so attractive in body, so corrupt in soul, and hence dialectically dangerous because of her very attractiveness.

But the repressed returned; among other instances, in twentieth-century Freudianism. In Freud's theory of bisexuality, the woman, "with her combination of masculine and feminine modes and her two sexual organs, one 'male' and one 'female,' is the general model of sexuality, and the male is only a particular variant of woman" (Culler 1983:171). This is where Freudianism unites with age-old Genesis, where bisexuality is precisely the starting point (for a critique of the Freudian concept of bisexuality, see Heath 1982).

The Emergence of the Human Body: Unaccomplishment

Let us follow, step by step, the construction of the character. The signs of the female body do not emerge right away. First, a sexless creature is formed. The first body, *the* body, unique and undivided, is the body of the earth creature, the work of Yahweh the potter. From 2:7 to 2:20 this creature has no name, no sex, and no activity. It emerges as a character-to-be, showing by what it has not, how a character should be. This first step is nothing more than the positing of existence of a potential character. The word *hā'ādām* is not attributed to it by Yahweh. It is used only by the narrator. Therefore, and because it carries the definite article, we can assume that it is not a proper name, but a common noun. As a minimal description of the concept it signifies, it is strikingly adequate. It is derived from the word used to indicate the material aspect of the earth, *hā'ădāmâ*. The pun is very pointed. As we will see, the creature is first of all characterized as *taken from*, differentiated from a larger environment. This principle of differentiation, which is the main characteristic of the creation in Genesis 1, is at the same time a basic semiotic principle. First the creature receives the signs of life. Borrowing from Yahweh's breath it receives life so that it receives living *nepeš*, becomes a living creature. The body is down-to-earth, life comes from the divine. This distinction is the occasion of the later idea of the split between body and soul. *Nepeš*, however, can mean neither soul nor spirit since that would attribute the same feature to animals (2:19). This life principle or totality of the self (Wolff 1974:10–25) is sometimes located in the blood (Lev. 17:11), which implies that it is anchored in the body.

The unfinished state of the earth creature, which we may call *clod*, both as a represented human being and as a literary character, is stressed by the word used to indicate it, which is a constant reminder of its modest origin and status: made of clay, it is as yet only a species, not an individual. It has no proper name yet. The word will become a name much later. As for action, the clod is still a puppet; entirely passive, it is put into the garden among the trees to grow. No features can be derived from this non-action.

In fact, the clod is put there twice, with the accounts of this event bracketing the growth: 8b–9–14–15. The second instance of this partial repetition (Rimmon-Kenan 1980), however, implies a future virtual activity (which will not be carried out): the tilling and keeping of the garden, a serving, respectful domination over nature. Thus, slowly, the specificity of human life emerges, but in a paradoxical way: a name not to be attributed yet, an activity not to be executed.

Trible (1978:80–140) stresses the sexually undifferentiated nature of this earth creature. Properly speaking, it cannot be said to be androgynous or bisexual, since sexuality is still to be created. Later versions do interpret it as such, though. In the younger, liturgical version of Gen. 1:26–27 Elohim create man as male and female in "their" own likeness— the verse gives evidence of an underlying androgynous image of the deity, as has been argued often enough (Leach 1983:33–66; O'Flaherty 1980)—and in Gen. 5:1–2 this androgyny is explicitly attributed to the being named *hā'ādām*, the earth creature itself. The use of the plural

pronoun in both 1:27 and 5:2 does not justify a singular, male interpretation of this instance of the earth creature. I will argue later that the
first creation story should not be considered as different from, let alone
alien to, the second one.

Apart from this intertextual evidence, there are at least two text-
internal arguments supporting the sexually undifferentiated nature of
hā'ādām within Gen. 2:4b–3; hence the latter comes to include the future
woman as well as the future man. If the word was to indicate the man
exclusively, then the prohibition in 2:16–17 of eating from the tree of
knowledge would not hold for the woman. However, in 3:2–3 she re-
peats the prohibition to the serpent. Second, the woman, then, would
not have been expelled from the garden, for in 3:22–23 Yahweh men-
tions only *hā'ādām*. Perhaps she still lives there . . . Both arguments can,
of course, be explained away. In the first case the man could have repeated the interdiction to the woman. This counterargument, however,
falls under L. C. Knights's case against questions like "How many children had Lady Macbeth?" (1964). It is a character/person confusion,
which fails to account for the semiotic status of character. The second
argument could be eliminated by the now already-stated domination of
man over woman (3:16): she just had to follow him. This counterargument is overdoing the text's sexism. There is no reason to assume that
the not-yet-instated Eve is textually eliminated altogether. Paradoxically,
Trible defends this reading (1978).

In the text of Gen. 2:4b–15, the signs construct a concept that contains
many features and at the same time lacks many. It contains features that
get lost later, like the narrow bond between this concept of humanity and
the earth, its absolute object-position and the moral innocence—and
impotence—it entails, its uniqueness. It lacks many other things, including the features that I have already indicated as constitutive of character: sex, name, action: responsibility. What makes readers assume this
creature is male? What, by another equally strange twist, makes them
assume that this mistaken priority implies superiority? Unable to read an
unfulfilled character, they supply the lacking features. Apparently they
have a concept of character in mind in which proper names and sexual
identity are inherent qualities.

The Emergence of the Female Body: Sexual Difference

The next step, after the signifying of sheer existence, is a further differentiation. The one singular creature becomes plural. If readers can
very easily supply the lacking features, the character itself can not. It is
Yahweh/God, not *hā'ādām*, who decides that "His" work is unfinished. "It

is not good for *hā'ādām* to be alone; I will make for it a companion corresponding to it" (2:18). The lack of sexual difference causes loneliness, but the being who lacks it cannot be aware of what it never had. It takes some time, however, before Yahweh understands that just to *add* beings will not do. The animals, outsiders as they are, do not *correspond* to the human creature. I will not elaborate upon the obviously sexist but common translation "a help fit for him." The "him" being already a faulty translation, the rest cannot make sense. Besides, such a translation misses the deep insight into the nature of sexuality that is worded in this text. At that, the word translated as "help" is too often used with reference to God to allow such a humble interpretation.

The animals are unfit and the different human being is not, because it is the tension between the *same* and the *different* that creates sexuality. The earth-being has to be severed, separated from part of itself, in order for the "other half" of what will then be left to come into existence.

A deep sleep makes the earth creature unconscious. It almost returns it into *hā'ādām*. This sleep is the death of the undifferentiated earth creature. It will emerge from it in differentiation.

The organ taken from it is supposed to be the *rib*. This word has been widely discussed. Some scholars think it means *side*. It could, then, be a euphemism for "belly," as "feet" often stands for "testicles." In that case, it could refer to the womb, an apparent reversal of sexual function that is not at all unthinkable in the case of this undifferentiated earth creature. A second suggestion, which is not incompatible with the previous one, is made by Oosten and Moyer (1982:80). They believe that Kramer (1961: 102–103) rightly connected this mytheme with the Sumeric myth of Enki in paradise. In this myth the goddess Nin-ti is created from Enki's rib. *Ti* means rib as well as "the making of life." Although the pun gets lost in Hebrew, the association may have made sense: the "mother of all living" who emerges in Gen. 3:20 is herself made from (a piece of) living material. Such a reversal of object and subject would be typical in mythological terms.

The verb used for Yahweh's forming of the earth creature was the specific verb for pottery; the verb used in 2:22 refers specifically to architecture and the construction of buildings. The action is both more difficult and more sophisticated, and it requires more differentiated material. The difference would indicate a higher level of creation. This idea is consistent with the poetics of the biblical conception of creation.

Just as the creation of humanity in the version of Gen. 1–2:4b is the climax of the creation of the world, the creation of humanity, as it is specified in this version under consideration, is performed in two progressive phases of perfection. This point refutes the first conclusion "Paul" draws from his first mistake. The material that is used no longer

consists of dust, of clay, but of bone and flesh, already enriched with
nepeš. The result is also higher: it is no longer an undifferentiated creature, but a sexual being, more precisely, a woman. "And Yahweh God
built the rib which he took from [undifferentiated] *hā'ādām* into woman
['*iššâ*]."

Of both words, '*îš* and '*iššâ*, which in this text indicate sexually differentiated being, '*iššâ*, woman, appears first. It is '*iššâ* who changes the
meaning of *hā'ādām* from earth-being into earth-man. In this semiotic
sense, the woman was first formed, then the man (*contra* "Paul").

But there is no reason to overstate her case. In the same way that the
man can come into being only by his differentiation from the woman, as
a next step in her creation, she has to be recognized as different, and
receive in her turn sexual identity from the man. Again, Yahweh dis-
poses of the not-yet-completed character that cannot act. He brings her
to *hā'ādām*, who, by the recognition of the other, assumes his own sexual
identity. The recognition of sexuality is worded in his poetry, the first
speech he utters. If the woman is the first to be signified, the man is the
first to speak. The attribution of speech to the man, this next step in the
creation of humanity, displays the thoroughly equalizing dialectic of the
process. Alter (1981:65–67) gives an interesting account of the poetics of
direct quotation in biblical narrative as he sees it, perhaps overgeneralizing. Quotation is one device of characterization and is, like naming,
thoroughly connected with the view of humanity frequently found in the
Bible. The distribution of speech and names among the different potential characters is therefore a relevant issue.

The lyric *hā'ādām* performs consists of three parts. First, he recognizes
the woman as part of the same *hā'ādām* of which he himself is a leftover:

> This, finally, bone of my bone
> and flesh of my flesh.

After the failures of 2:19–20, this is a joyful celebration of their common
nature, their brother- and sisterhood. The man is, then, not the parent
from whom the woman is born, as another obvious reading would have
it, but, if we stick to these inappropriate family metaphors, rather, her
brother. He is the son of *hā'ādām*, she, the daughter. This interpretation
of the first humans as not really the very first is much more congenial
with other creation myths, in which a first being, symbiotic with earth
and/or heaven, is replaced by a second or even a third one. Zeus is a case
in point.

After the recognition of their similarity, *hā'ādām* the Second celebrates
difference. The phrase creates a problem of interpretation:

> This shall be called woman ['*iššâ*]
> because from man ['*îš*] was taken this.

A problem here is the use of the sexually marked noun '*îš*. Lévinas (1973) discusses the importance of this noun for the formation of the idea that the very essence of femininity is in woman's origin as after-thought: "la féminité même de la femme est dans cet initial après-coup" (The very femininity of woman is in this initial afterthought). (On Lévi-nas's view of women in the Bible, see also Chalier 1982.) Indeed, it would be more convenient for me if the noun *hā'ādām* had been used, so that I could assume it was used in the first, undifferentiated sense. There are two ways out. A first possibility would be that after allotropy, the change of physical properties within the same substance, the man retrospectively assumes that he always had this sexual identity. He focalizes his earlier version from his actual state. Just as adults have no memories of their early childhood, during which they were not yet full subjects, let alone their prenatal life, the man understandably cannot imagine that he was once a nonsexual being. This need not make us angry at him, nor at the narrator who quotes his words in this way. The analogy just suggests an interpretative frame, the psychoanalytical one, on which I cannot dwell here but which is obviously relevant. Already, the word *hā'ādām* is defi-nitely lost to its previous meaning, as subsequent readings show.

However plausible and, indeed, acceptable this explanation is, there is another equally plausible possibility. The phrase "taken from" does not mean "made out of" but "taken away from" in the sense of "differenti-ated from." The man, then, is right. Out of *hā'ādām* Yahweh made '*iššâ* and '*îš* by separating the one from the other. Similarly, in the previous phase of the creation, Yahweh made *hā'ādām* by separating it from the rest of the earth, *hā'ādāmâ* which by that separation changed radically: its unity was broken, it became less chaotic, it lost a potential humanity, and it acquired a potential caretaker and master. The same pun stresses difference in similarity. Therefore the same root was needed. This inter-pretation of the creation/differentiation of the sexes is thus more consis-tent with the overall conception of creation in Genesis.

After unity and separation, the narration sums up; sexuality is a return to unity. Yet more than that:

> Therefore, a man leaves his father and his mother
> and cleaves to his woman
> and they become one flesh.

Love resembles death: just as death will be presented (3:19) as a return to origin, love is presented here as a return to the union of one flesh. But love *is not* death. Analogy is not identity. Love, here, is not lethal. The idea holds the following elements:

—it is the man who joins the woman;
—love is a return to an earlier stage ("therefore");
—parents are mentioned.

The "invention" of parents as the species of people to be left behind is a logical consequence of what has happened. A couple was formed by the separation out of unity; "therefore" the initial state of unity will permanently trouble man with nostalgia; the same unity will be sought and the same separation will follow. Hence, history starts here. The narrator generalizes, foresees, and prospectively retrospects: he installs chronology.

The man as speaker, creating history and the succession of generations, carries out the next step in the creation of literary character. Promoted as he is from an undifferentiated, sexless creature to Everyman, he still has no proper name, no individuality. But he does, now, occupy the historical position of the son-becoming-father.

We can now return to "Paul's" first claim. Although it is possible to assume that, strictly speaking, the woman was the first to exist, since she was the first to be signified, I see nothing of interest in such a claim. The biblical poetics of creation does not assign primacy to chronological priority. Moreover, such a claim rests on a priority of signs over the subject, which also is not consistent with the poetics of creation as we see it at work in Genesis. Creation is a *verbal* activity. The subject of signification, therefore, has a power analogous to the creator's power. In the case that preoccupies us here, while the woman may be the first signified character, the man is the first signifying subject. If the woman is differentiated first, the man is the first to recognize sexual difference. I want to put forward the contention that this distribution of semiotic roles implies a dialectic equivalence of sign and subject, which mutually constitute each other. Man and woman, then, were created at the same time.

This argument makes a case against those comments which assume a contradiction between the two creation stories. The Bible often includes several factually contradictory but hermeneutically complementary versions of one event. Alter (1981:142–43), for example, following the commonly accepted philological conclusions, distinguishes between the realistic (2:4b–25) and the theological (1–2:4a) versions of the creation. The editors, Alter claims, assumed that God created man and woman equal (Gen. 1) but, on the other hand, saw that in society there was not such equality. They therefore included the "sexist" version of Genesis 2. Alter's view seems plausible insofar as later interpretations have turned Gen. 2 into the sexist story it has become. The "equal rights" version has, then, to be explained away. But its return in 5:1–2 makes the repression problematic. Alter's defense of the paradoxical coherence of Genesis was, however, uncalled for. The text as it stands does not contradict Genesis 1 at all. In fact, it provides a specified narration of what events are included in the idea that "God created them male and female." This synecdochical composition turns Genesis 1–2 into one coherent creation story. Coherence is not, in my view, an absolute ontological or structural literary category; on the contrary. I conceive it as a reading device and subsequently as a device for the interpretation of editorial policy (see Bal Ms. for a discussion). In the present case I want to claim that the eventual authors of the later first version were not presenting a theological counterstatement to the second and older one. They were good readers and wrote a piece that retrospectively completed the imaginary representation of this particular conception of creation through differentiation. As we will see now, the same compositional principle turns Genesis 1–3, and subsequently the whole book, into a coherent story. For, similarly, Genesis 3 will elaborate laterally upon the implications of the other specification of Gen. 1:27: he created them to his likeness. And that is a different story.

The Emergence of Activity: Sin?

In the next episode, being and action mutually constitute each other. In its reception, features are drawn from action, and action is supposed to be based on features.

Phase One: *Awareness of the Body*

Between ahistorical existence and the beginning of history, the last sentence of Genesis 2 can be considered as a transition: "Now they both were naked, *hā'ādām* and his woman, and they were not ashamed." Whether or not the so-called Yahwist editors have combined the stories of the creation and the story of the fall, initially different, the collocation is significant. But the latter is still a different story, representing a different phase in the unfolding of narrative as a genre.

The sentence supplies information that prepares the ground for the events to happen. It states the duality of the future characters, and it maps the semantic field of the story: nakedness versus shame. The semantic field will unfold as follows.

Before the fall, "naked" is the opposite of "ashamed": naked, they do not know shame: naked ↔ ashamed. They are like innocent children. The implication on the left side of Greimas's semiotic square (Greimas 1970) evolves into the right side, where "not naked" implies "dressed," and dress is caused by shame, so that the implication is

The awareness of nudity immediately seems to entail shame. The complete square runs, then, as diagrammed in Table 8.

Table 8

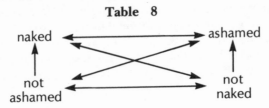

After the story of the creation of the body, after that of sexually differentiated bodies, comes the story of the development from nonawareness to awareness of the body. It is the first "inner-view" representation of feelings, and hence a step further in the construction of character. But awareness and shame are not immediately related. The first mention of shame, however ambiguous, is made by the man in 3:10 when he replies to Yahweh that they hid because they were naked. It is Yahweh's appearance, not nakedness itself, that gives shame. In fact, it is the *confrontation* between characters that establishes this influential semantic turmoil. Confrontation, indeed, is the narrative aspect unfolded in this episode.

Phase Two: The Possibility of Action

The first being to appear in this phase of the development of character is the serpent. It is an ambivalent creature, ontologically, morally, as well as narratologically. It is an animal, but it talks. It is the first being to confront another one, the differentiated woman, but it uses the plural verb form; hence it addresses the man, too. Woman and serpent are both still generalizations of a species or sex, but the confrontation (Barthes 1977) brings them a step closer to the status of character and promotes the narrative status of the fabula. The serpent, then, is the first potential character to open the possibility of *action* in this story (Bremond 1972).

The main feature of the serpent is slyness. That feature is morally ambivalent. It holds cleverness, but not necessarily deceit. The serpent displays the feature in its speech: "Did God really say, you shall not eat from every tree in the garden?" Presenting God's interdiction as so absolute, so tyrannical, the serpent incites revolt. But it is not so easy to eliminate this "every" as a lie. In 2:16–17 Yahweh said seemingly the opposite: *hā'ādām* was allowed to eat of every tree except one. Let us see which trees are then left.

Phase Three: Choice

In 2:9 the available trees are described: Yahweh "caused to grow every tree pleasant to look at and good to eat," thus introducing the senses of sight and taste. But then the text seems to give a description of those pleasant trees: "the tree of life in the midst of the garden, and the tree of the knowledge of good and evil." Does the collection of "every tree" consist of only two species, or just one? This passage has understandably given rise to much discussion. Westermann (1966) assumes that there is only one tree, which is twice described because two versions of the story have been combined here. The phrase would mean, then: "the tree of life . . . namely, the tree of knowledge." This interpretation draws support from the woman's reply to the serpent. She describes the forbidden tree, the tree of knowledge, as "the tree in the midst of the garden." Extratextual support might also be drawn from mythological tradition. In many myths there is a tree of life guarded by a serpent (Eliade 1964: 310–24). Neither type of argument is relevant in relation to the formation of the myth based on *this* text. The problem to be dealt with, in this interpretation, is the relation between "life" and "knowledge of good and evil." If, as is highly plausible, the knowledge alluded to includes sexual knowledge, this problem is only too apparent. The two descriptions become synonymous, and life, or immortality, has the same value as knowledge. Oosten and Moyer (1982:72) suggest that the moral attribute "of good and evil" may have been added later. This would imply that the moral judgment on sexuality is a later invention.

The other possibility, that is, the existence of two specific trees, draws support from the end of the story. Angry because man has gained the knowledge that makes him near to divine, Yahweh expels him from the garden and appoints a guardian for the tree of life. The interpretation by the woman in 3:2–3, then, would be mistaken. This alleged error has often been cited as evidence of stupidity, a feature eagerly attributed to her, but cannot account for the ongoing discussion between her and the serpent, in which what is at stake is knowledge and divinity, and not life.

Also, one may wonder why Yahweh would suddenly start to worry about a tree that until then had not been prohibited.

There is a third possibility. There may indeed be two different trees, one offering immortality and one supplying knowledge. If, as the synonymic use of the verb *yada* for "to know" and "to have sex" suggests, this knowledge includes sexual knowledge, it does indeed supply immortality, not to the individual but to the species. The confusion of the two trees by the woman is then not only understandable, but even very wise. Therefore I disagree with Trible (1978:119) when she proposes an unnecessarily easy theological solution to the differences in the three descriptions of the tree (2:17; 3:3; 3:11). She explains them as evidence of their utter unimportance: the tree is just the tree of Divine Command. I would suggest rather that the three versions hold a progressive and dialectical circumscription of what is at stake. In 2:17 it is knowledge, including sexual knowledge with its consequence for life; in 3:3 the idea of death as the other side of life is mentioned; in 3:11 sheer disobedience or, in another sense, emancipation from blind command provides the passage from one to the other: once sexuality is accepted, humanity can do without impossible immortality.

The serpent's next statement, then, is not at variance with Yahweh's argument for the interdiction. Yahweh has said (2:17): "When you eat from it, you will surely die," while the serpent retorts: "indeed you will not die . . . your eyes will be opened and you will be like God, knowing good and evil." Indeed, sexual knowledge, be it morally colored or not, does "open your eyes" and makes you both die and not die. It makes you live on in the children it allows you to produce. It creates history: the chronological succession of generations in life and death, against which Judah revolted. Also, "the woman saw that good was the tree." In the Hebrew Bible the verb "to see" has a strong connotation of truth: to see is to have insight into what really is, behind false appearances or incomplete information. It is "desired to make one wise." The wisdom alluded to cannot be but the acceptance of the human condition, including death, and the continuity of history that it allows. What features does this entail for the woman? We are far removed, here, from the belly-oriented stupidity this woman is so often blamed for. On the contrary, she is open to reality and ready to adopt it.

Although it is only directly relevant for the issues at stake in this chapter, it is illuminating to examine the tree symbolism further back in the anthropology of prehistorical taboos. Only then can we fully acknowledge the importance of the different descriptions of the tree here. Reed (1975) gives an account of the origins of totemism, which includes sexual and food taboos. The basic principle of the system is the fact that no distinction existed between the two drives. This explains the curious fact that the commonly acknowledged sexual issue of the prohibition of the tree is "symbolized" by food. In Reed's way of thinking, this would be a wrong way of putting it. The tree, or rather its fruit, does not represent or symbolize sexuality; it includes it. Both food and sexuality are aspects of life and of the possibility of its maintenance. Both have to be protected, by totemization, from life-threatening misuse. The knowledge of how to avoid such misuse is rightly indicated as knowledge of "good and evil."

What, then, is the misuse that this knowledge can help to avoid? According to Reed (1975:279), the prohibition was basically a taboo against cannibalism. The idea may shock those who fail to understand the nature of cannibalism and its connection with sex taboos. Cannibalism is simply a *lack of differentiation*. Eating your own kind (or mating with your own kin) is threatening for the species because it exhausts the kind. It is plausible that primitive man could hardly distinguish between human and (other) animal species; his own clan versus the other beings was the only distinction he could make. The taboo on a certain animal could help him to learn to make distinctions. So much for Reed's general theory. Whatever one may think of its status—it cannot be but highly speculative—one of its aspects is familiar to us: the problematic of *difference*.

Reed's interpretation of the Eden prohibition is, however, incomplete. It accounts for the prohibition itself but not for the transgression. The interest of this (too succinctly rendered) theory of totemism lies in the possibility of accommodating the various descriptions of the tree(s) as well as the meaningfulness of the transgression. The tension between "every tree" and the poor collection of available trees described in 2:9 is resolved when we consider the distinction between "every tree" and any specific tree as the main point at stake. The general idea is that as soon as the humans know how to distinguish, they will not eat (or touch, as the woman, significantly, adds) anything harmful. But next we must distinguish in our turn between Yahweh's and the woman's view, according to their respective relations to the human species. In view of this learning process, Yahweh the teacher prohibited a tree, in order that the humans should learn differentiation, and he specifically prohibited the tree of knowledge. Why this one? Because it would make them like God. This is a matter of focalization. In God's eyes, eating the divine substance would be eating one's own kind. For the woman, the latter argument does not count, because the humans were not yet divine. The knowledge made them divine precisely because it implied the capacity to distinguish, hence to *avoid*, eating one's own kind. The decision to strive for that capacity, that is for the wisdom mentioned in 3:7, displayed the success of Yahweh's teaching. The prohibition itself implied the possibility of transgression, a motivated transgression justified because it was based on the very capacity for differentiation that was at issue.

But if the serpent was right in its promise of wisdom instead of death, was Yahweh then wrong after all? This interpretation rests on the equal position of the serpent and Yahweh in relation to truth. Both are sly, withholding information but not actually lying. Yahweh stresses one aspect, mortality, the serpent the other, knowledge, of the same idea. Both, in collaboration, trick the humans into accepting the unavoidable, that is, into renouncing the childish fantasy of individual immortality. The woman, interpreting the words of both actors in relation to the interest of human life, makes her own decision. If, as many Middle Eastern myths have it, the serpent, which is the representative of immortality because of its capacity to renew its skin, is God's helper as the guardian of the tree of life, then our serpent does an excellent job. Also, the serpent with its double tongue, evolving into the dragon with its flaming tongues, may be read as the same creature as the cherubim with flaming sword of Gen. 3:24. It has similar features and a similar function.

This passage is one of the most problematic ones, because here the anthropological issue has been buried so long under theological considerations that it seems impossible to accept the literary status of God. For example, in spite of her feminist and literary intentions, Trible is from here on, I am afraid, taken in by her religious feelings, which make her overrate the character of Yahweh. She fails to take his/her literary status seriously when she assumes, for example, that Yahweh's recognition of the human couple's divine likeness (3:22) is an ironic reversal of what he really thinks (1978:136). This may save his divine superiority but does not account for his fear and defensiveness in 3:22–24. Trible's mistake is that she exempts Yahweh from the mutually structuring semiotic relations between all the characters. She misses the analogy principle.

Phase Four: Action

Serpent, tree, and deity are thus defined in relation to the first narrative action performed in the myth. The tree, as a source of temptation, the serpent as the actual tempter, and God as the prohibitor of the action, are equally endowed with narrative functions. They share the actantial position of the *destinateur*: they all play minor but indispensable parts in the fabula. It is their status as structurally related characters that the woman calls into being by the action in relation to which they occupy this position. For what happens?

The woman paradoxically realizes the creation of humanity in God's likeness and, by the same token, the creation of literary character, in which God is created in man's likeness. It was the likeness to God that the serpent presented to her as the main charm of the tree. This likeness included the free will to act, which was implied in the interdiction itself. Jealousy about the possible equivalence is alleged as Yahweh's motive for the interdiction. Yahweh's later reaction proves the serpent was right. The author and his characters turn out to be equal antagonists in the fabula in which the author is dramatized. The woman promotes her own status in the narrative. Her disobedience is the first independent act, which makes her powerful as a character. Not only has she the power to make the man eat, hence to make him know (her), and disobey in his turn. But also she manages to turn the almighty God of Genesis 1 into a character with equal status, equal features, equal feelings to the others. From now on this creating Spirit (Gen. 1:2) has a body; one that seeks the freshness of the garden, strolls in it and looks for its fellow inhabitants; he has a personality that makes him angry and even, later (3:22), afraid. He is no longer in a position to "take" and "put" the human objects wherever he wishes. Speech becomes dialogue, action, confrontation. The relationship between them is now basically horizontal, both in terms of actantial power and in terms of space. It had to be like that: exclusive power, in Genesis 1, prevented narrativization. The only act performed there was the semiotization of chaos. Shared power, included in the creation of male/female to "His" (capital "H") likeness, installs confrontation, struggle, events, time: history and narrative.

The Emergence of Character: Sorrow

The next and final step is the attribution of the proper name. It becomes possible after the attribution of definite, restrictive features. As we have seen, the woman and the man, transgressing Yahweh's prohibition, established the structural network of actantial positions. The woman was the leading actant; she did not exactly sin, she opted for reality. Therefore it is not obvious that Yahweh's reaction should be considered as a punishment. It seems more plausible to take it as an explicit spelling out of the consequences of the human option, as another representation of the reality of human life.

The episode consists of a series of interpellations. As the other side of speech, interpellation adds another trait to the construction of character. Interpellating them, Yahweh acknowledges responsibility, and hence the character positions of each actant. First, he addresses the man. The expression of shame betrayed the man: "Who told you that you were naked?" Indeed, the awareness of nakedness was the immediate consequence of the acquisition of knowledge. Speaking and spoken to, focalizing (his shame) and focalized, acting, the man now fully participates in the narrative process. The man tries to blame both the woman and Yahweh, who gave her to him. Then Yahweh turns to the woman, who blames the serpent. The serpent, then, is addressed next, but not as a full subject able to speak. Yahweh immediately curses it, without asking any question. Thus he limits its position as a character. It is thrown back into its state of speechless animal. The content of the curse is simply the subsequent realistic image of serpents as crawling and dangerous animals.

The woman is not cursed. The content of Yahweh's words to her is actually not even presented as the consequence of what she has done—let alone as a punishment. Here, again, we seem to have a faithful depiction of reality. But how real is reality?

> I will greatly multiply your labor and your childbearing
> in pain you will bring forth children
> and your '*iš* is your desire
> and he will rule over you. (3:16)

The word "multiply" is a little strange, since no children have been born yet. The use of the word "labor," repeated in the address to the man, suggests that this is a distribution of labor among the sexes: the man will work for food, the woman for children. The establishment of sexual roles is carried out in these lines (3:16–19). Now, the second part of this speech is most disturbing for feminists. It is tempting to claim that the almighty "equal rights" God of 1:27 is developing here into an ordinary male character, affected himself by the invention of sexual roles he is acting out. There is still one surprise detail, then. The relation of desire, which, as the precondition of pregnancy, could be expected to be mentioned first, only follows the mention of labor, the consequence of pregnancy. This suggests that the relation of domination comes up as an afterthought, judged less important, perhaps less fatal, than the pain of labor. The hierarchy would then be based on a different degree of realism. This idea slightly shades the image of Yahweh the male character.

Oosten and Moyer (1982:83) propose a more far-reaching idea. They draw attention to Gen. 4:7. In an entirely alien context, namely when Yahweh explains to Cain why his offering has been rejected, we suddenly read:

> and unto you [shall be] his desire
> and you shall rule over him.

Indeed, in 4:7 the phrase doesn't make sense at all. Therefore, the authors suggest that initially it was part of Yahweh's speech to the woman in

Gen. 3:16–19; later editors did not notice the logic of reciprocity, because reality did not exactly display equal rights between the sexes; hence, they displaced the lines.

The suggestion is attractive, since it undercuts one argument against the misogynist interpretation of the text. Two text-internal arguments support it, even if they are not conclusive. First, the man has explicitly expressed male desire in his celebration of love (2:24), and it would make sense for Yahweh to stress its negative side here, just as he reverses the gentle "keeping and tilling" of the earth into hard labor. Second, Yahweh is clearly more severe on the man than on the woman. He explicitly blames him and indirectly curses him by cursing the earth from which he was taken and to which he shall return. It seems plausible, therefore, that he would subordinate the man as well. The displacement can then be seen as an *Entstellung*, a distortion and a dislocation at the same time (Weber 1982).

Even if this philological detail can influence our evaluation of the ideological flavor of the mytheme under consideration, it certainly is of minor importance in relation to its main tendency. For, with a narrative logic proper to these stories, Yahweh has carried out the next phase in the formation of characters by attributing to them, as a complement to their actantial position, bundles of features that determine the realm of their future actions and limit their possibilities. He does that in a way that does not inspire our gratitude: by fixing sexual roles. As an ideological agent, he creates "those identities of man and woman, the fictions of oppression" against which modern critique claims to struggle (Heath 1982:168).

The relations between the sexes are fixed in terms of the semantic axes of fertility and domination, and are, as such, arbitrary. Fertility necessitates labor, and domination presupposes desire as its precondition, according to Yahweh's statement. It is true that modern medical science still maintains the reality of the idea of unavoidable labor, but the relation between desire and domination hardly seems "natural." Power and domination establish the organization of social life, while, more specifically, the distribution of roles in reproduction, where woman produces children and man, food, organizes work.

Looking back to the creation of sexual difference, it is striking that the difference there was established as an empty, purely relational category, more or less in the same sense as de Saussure's networks of oppositions without positive terms. Neither the woman nor the man is described as anatomically typical. We are far removed from today's conception of sexuality as anatomical difference: "In our culture, we refer to the classificatory divisions based on anatomy as sexual divisions. This is because anatomy has become synonymous with sexual identity and activity" (Coward 1982:280). Mentioning labor and desire, Yahweh predicts this evolution. It is in this episode only, and not before, that characters come into being endowed with "relevant" semantic features; in other words, that the relevance of their features is fixed. If there is a sexist ideology inscribed in this text, it is not until this passage that it can be pointed to.

Since the characters are completed now, they can receive the label that makes them memorable: proper name. It is, again, the woman who is the first and only character explicitly named. Again, this priority in the formation of character is balanced by the fact that the man is the first and only subject of naming. As we have seen, the word hā'ādām had been used by the narrator as self-evident; the serpent was only indicated by its generic name; 'îš and 'iššâ were nouns used for sexual differentiation. Eve, ḥawwâ, a name that means, as her mate says, "the mother of all living," is solemnly applied to 'iššâ in view of her sexual and social role. The name is, like many biblical names, motivated and hence descriptive. The man, in giving her this particular name, determines the character further: Eve is imprisoned in motherhood. There is no more queston of the sexual attraction celebrated in 2:23–24.

Confronted with this dubious title of honor, "Paul's" violent reaction is highly suspect. Indeed, in stressing the prohibition against women teaching, he seems to react to this motherly function inscribed in the proper name. At the same time, the collocation of the inferior body and moral inferiority stands in opposition to motherhood: "Notwithstanding she shall be saved in childbearing," continues "Paul" in 1 Tim. 2:15. The question arises: do women deserve contempt in spite of, or because of, their motherhood? Christian morality, echoed in the invention of "pure" motherhood in the character of Mary, the anti-Eve (whose virginity, of course, is mythical; see Warner 1976), holds the former; psychoanalysis, in stressing the problems the child has to live through, the too-binding relation with the mother, suggests the latter. The very invention of Mary, sadistic as it is in the requirements it imposed on women, paradoxically shows the impossibility of overcoming the tension between the two positions. Mary was supposed to correct Eve, in that she was the "pure" mother, but the very notion is self-contradictory. According to her image, woman is bad in spite of motherhood, because she cannot but fail to limit herself to it. Eve, Mary's presumably negative counterpart, had in fact a better start, representing both sexuality and motherhood. The man, however, fails to appreciate that: after his celebration of love, now forgotten, he exclusively stresses the other side of woman: motherhood. Thus Eve, starting in wholeness, is now condemned to predict Mary.

But there is more. The proper name in narrative can be structurally related not only to the features of the character itself but also to other names. Hamon (1983:107–49) studies the system of proper names in

Zola's novels. He comes up with the term *actant phonétique*, which he defines as follows (122): "a constant group of phonemes, characterized by its recurrence and its stability . . . a fundamental unity situated between the general signifier of the text, that which we have called its rumor(s), and the particular proper name of the character-actor." The interest of such a concept is its structural aspect. Avoiding pointless and arbitrary interpretations of isolated phonetic features, a procedure we cannot dream of anyway in the case of ancient texts, it draws attention to the construction of relations between characters. This seems to make sense in the case of the Hebrew Bible, where naming is a meaningful act meant to establish the relation between the character and its main feature. The puns we met with earlier, especially *hā'ădāmâ/hā'ādām*, suggest such a relation between characters. The earth is left behind as a non-character, and the future character Adam will return to it later. In this respect, the fact that the woman, as the first representative of a sexually differentiated human being, is the climax of the creation, and the fact that she is appointed as the future creator/provider of "all living," may very well be signified in the resemblance between her name and Yahweh's, HW being the phonetic actant that opposes the creators to the creatures, signified by DM. Again, this argument is not meant to imply a female superiority but a functional analogy between the two creative forces. Adam, by giving the woman that name, is the very character who stresses this creative function. In his address to the man, Yahweh in his turn highlights Adam's functional relationship to the earth, which, presented both as an antagonistic and as a sympathetic force, is endowed with the actantial position of the opponent. Hence the four are cross-determined: Adam relates Eve to Yahweh; Yahweh relates Adam to earth. The characters are now completed: interrelated, endowed with features, their names make them memorable. Thus, at the end of the story, the myth of Eve begins.

The Effect of Naming

Naming, as we have seen, is the labeling of the character that completes its formation. But its complete state does not necessarily imply all its previous states. Gen. 1–3 provides ample evidence to the contrary. The confrontation between the two myths allows us to understand the ideological effect of the named character.

Hamon (1983:107) describes the effect of the proper name as follows:

> To study a character is to be able to name it. To act, for the character, is also, first, to be able to spell out, address, call and name the other characters of the narrative. Reading is to be able to fix one's attention and one's memory on stable points in the text, the proper names.

These remarks interestingly corroborate the findings of the present analysis. While studying the text it has been impossible to name the character Eve until the very end. To have done so would have disfigured the design of the text. Second, naming has been the man's prerogative. This enhances the paradox of semiotic creation: he was the first to name, which, according to Hamon, is a condition for action. But she was the first to be named, hence, to be "the other character" indispensable for his being a character at all. Thus they mutually create each other, as different, in a different act.

As for the third aspect of Hamon's statement, the slow emergence of the proper name has caused a serious reading problem that has compulsively stimulated readers to adopt the retrospective fallacy that I hold largely responsible for the ideological uses of the text—for what happened to our test reader "Paul." He started at the end, that is, at the proper name. This approach enabled him to "fix his memory." It implies the possibility of combining the name with the sexist myth that is already attached to it ("it is the same Eve"), and that is motivated by, and reinforces, his contempt for women. He endowed the named character with those features from the previous story which nourished that contempt for women, namely, the "secondary" creation of her body and the "primary" disobedience in her action. He fixed them together as if they belonged to the same being, unproblematically. In the case of a developmental story, however, starting at the end means losing sight of the development. In the linear reading, the possibility that these features are self-evident is questioned by the very concept of development.

The construction of character has followed a specific line in the story. First its existence was posited, but then it was not yet a sexual being. Then it was sexually differentiated, addressed, and successively endowed with different aspects of subjectivity. It became the subject of awareness, hence of focalization; of speech; of possible action; of choice; and of actual action. It was characterized by description. Then, and only then, it was named: Adam the man, Eve the woman. "Paul" entirely missed that construction. Hence, he missed the point of the creation story. For that point is, simply, creation, by differentiation—of humanity, of character.

AFTERWORD

In all the love stories discussed, love is represented as lethal—at some point, at least; not throughout the stories, and not in the same way in each story. David's love for Bathsheba brought about Uriah's death. Samson's love for Delilah killed him. Ruth seems the exception that proves the rule, but what happened to her first husband, what to Naomi's, what to Orpah's? They all died, for unspecified reasons. Was their case similar to those of Tamar's husbands, who died more explicitly because of sex? Eve, the eternal paradigm, brought death over the entire species. She did not invent death but she accepted it. Should we conclude, then, that the ideology of the Hebrew Bible has it that women should be avoided, that love kills the man who is its victim? Modern readings of the stories seem to believe it does.

On closer inspection, the texts can be read differently. But what does "closer inspection" mean, and what is the difference? The idea of lethal love is indeed expressed in the stories. The question is, by whom? There lies the interest of the focus on the subject as a concept in narrative theory. The repression of the subject in Genette's narratology on the one hand, and its conflation with the individual in other critical theories on the other, has been considered as symptomatic of its very importance. Focusing on the different subject-positions involved in narrative has allowed me to differentiate between the status of various expressions. That is how it was possible to notice both the idea of lethal love and its problematic background, its struggle against other views of love, its insecurity. If David kills Uriah for love, we don't need to assume that the overall ideology of the text agrees. And this for the simple reason that there is no overall ideology of the text.

The type of narratological analysis advocated in this study provides insight into what the text presents as problematic. Love is not lethal, but there is a problem for some people who think it is: such is the statement I have read in the stories, if statements there were at all. What went wrong in the history of the reception of these stories is precisely the repression of the problem, hence, of the heterogeneous ideology of the text, which had to be turned into a monolithic one. Textual subjectivity had to be replaced with *the* subject of the text.

There can be no doubt that my interpretations are thoroughly anachronistic if one wishes to find the "original meaning" of the stories. I hope it has been clear enough that such was not my purpose. Quite the contrary. My readings present an alternative to other readings, not a "correct," let alone the "only possible" interpretation of what the texts "really say." Texts trigger readings; that is what they are: the occasion of a reaction. The feeling that there is a text in support of one's view makes texts such efficient ideological weapons. Every reading is different from, and in contact with, the text. The stories have made me think about what ancient people possibly dealt with when they were thinking about love and women. What I assume they thought is what my interpretations are about. If one can easily disagree with my readings, if only because one does not share my interests, at least I will have raised possibilities that can make people think in their turn. Breaking open the too-monolithic readings projected on the Hebrew love stories in order to make others believe that life, love, and women are what one wants them to be: such was one purpose of this book. Showing that the tools of literary theory can be used not only for "neutral" descriptions but also to make political readings more plausible and understandable was another one. This politicizing of theoretical terms has been carefully argued in the first chapter, blatantly applied in the others. I wanted to suggest that this practice makes theory more relevant and more interesting. I was trying to answer the legitimate question: what is the point? Through the patient elaboration of the set of critical terms, a critique of previous readings, and the construction of my own, I came up with the answer: the point is that there is none, at least not a single one; the point of literary analysis is that there is no truth, and that this contention can be reasonably argued. And where the truth is absent, women can creep in, and rewrite themselves back into the history of ideology.

REFERENCES

Alphen, Ernst van. 1987. *Bang voor schennis? Inleiding in de ideologiekritiek.* Utrecht: HES.

Alter, Robert. 1981. *The Art of Biblical Narrative.* New York: Basic Books.

Angenot, Mark. 1980. *Les champions des femmes.* Montréal: Presses de l'Université du Québec.

Bal, Mieke. 1980. "Narrativité et manipulation." *Degrés* 8.

———. 1985. *Narratology: Introduction to the Theory of Narrative.* Toronto: University of Toronto Press.

———. 1986. *Femmes imaginaires. L'ancien testament au risque d'une narratologie critique.* Utrecht: HES; Montréal: HMH; Paris: Nizet.

———. 1987. "Myth à la lettre." In *Discourse in Psychoanalysis and Literature,* ed. Shlomith Rimmon-Kenan. London and New York: Methuen.

———. 1988. *Murder and Difference: Gender, Genre, and Scholarship on Sisera's Death.* Bloomington: Indiana University Press.

———. Ms. "Death and Dissymmetry: The Politics of Coherence in Judges."

Barthes, Roland. 1957. *Mythologies.* Paris: Editions du Seuil. Translated by Richard Howard, under the title *The Eiffel Tower and other Mythologies.* New York: Hill and Wang, 1979.

———. 1968. "L'effet du réel." *Communications* 11.

———. 1970. *S/Z.* Paris: Editions du Seuil. (*S/Z.* London: Jonathan Cape, 1974).

———. 1974. *S/Z.* Translated by Richard Miller. New York: Hill & Wang.

———. 1977. "Introduction to the Structural Analysis of Narratives." In *Image-Music-Text.* London: Methuen.

Belsey, Catherine. 1980. *Critical Practice.* London: Methuen.

Benveniste, Emile. 1966. *Problèmes de linguistique générale.* Paris: Gallimard.

Bettelheim, Bruno. 1976. *The Uses of Enchantment.* New York: Alfred A. Knopf.

Bremond, Claude. 1972. *Logique du récit.* Paris: Editions du Seuil.

Brooks, Peter. 1984. *Reading for the Plot: Design and Intention in Narrative.* New York: Alfred A. Knopf; Oxford: Oxford University Press.

Chalier, Cathérine. 1982. *Figures du féminin. Lecture d'Emmanuel Lévinas.* Paris: La nuit surveillée.

Chase, Cynthia. 1986. *Decomposing Figures: Rhetorical Readings in the Romantic Tradition.* Baltimore: Johns Hopkins University Press.

Coward, Rosalind. 1982. *Patriarchal Precedents: Sexuality and Social Relations.* London: Routledge and Kegan Paul.

Coward, Rosalind, and John Ellis. 1977. *Language and Materialism: Developments in Semiology and the Theory of the Subject.* London: Routledge and Kegan Paul.

Culler, Jonathan. 1981. *The Pursuit of Signs: Semiotics, Literature, Deconstruction.* London: Routledge and Kegan Paul.

———. 1983. *On Deconstruction: Theory and Criticism after Structuralism.* London: Routledge and Kegan Paul.

Dällenbach, Lucien. 1977. *Le récit spéculaire. Essai sur la mise en abyme.* Paris: Editions du Seuil.

Delay, Jean. 1973. *La jeunesse d'André Gide.* Paris: Payot.

Derrida, Jacques. 1972. *Positions.* Paris: Minuit.

———. 1976. *Of Grammatology.* Translated by Gayatri Chakravorty Spivak. Baltimore: Johns Hopkins University Press.

Dijk, Teun A. van. 1977. *Text and Context.* London and New York: Longman.

Eco, Umberto. 1976. *A Theory of Semiotics.* Bloomington: Indiana University Press.

Edwards, Ann. 1969. *A Child's Bible.* London: Pan Books Ltd.

Eliade, Mircea. 1964. *Traité de l'histoire des religions.* Paris: Payot.

Evenhuis, Gertie, and Nico Bouhuijs. 1978. *Dromen van vrede. Verhalen uit het Oude Testament.* Amsterdam: Ploegsma.

Fabian, Johannes. 1983. *Time and the Other: How Anthropology Makes its Object.* New York: Columbia University Press.

Felman, Shoshana. 1980. *Le scandale du corps parlant. Don Juan avec Austin ou la Séduction en deux langues.* Paris: Editions du Seuil.

Fish, Stanley. 1971. "Surprised by Sin." In *The Reader in Paradise Lost.* Berkeley: University of California Press.

Fokkelman, J. P. 1981. *King David: Narrative Art and Poetry in the Books of Samuel.* Assen: van Gorcum.

Forster, E. M. 1954. *Aspects of the Novel.* New York: Harcourt Brace Jovanovich.

Freud, Sigmund. 1957. "On the Universal Tendency to Debasement in the Sphere of Love" (1912). Standard Edition, vol. XI, 177–89; "The Taboo of Virginity" (1918). Standard Edition, vol. XI, 191–206. New York: Norton.

Genette, Gérard. 1973. *Figures III.* Paris: Editions du Seuil. Translated by Jane Lewin, under the title *Narrative Discourse: An Essay on Method.* Ithaca: Cornell University Press, 1980.

Gennep, Arnold van. 1960. *The Rites of Passage* (1909). Translated by Monika B. Vizedon and Gabrielle L. Caffee. Chicago: University of Chicago Press.

Greimas, Algirdas Julien. 1965. *Sémantique structurale.* Paris: Larousse. Translated by Daniele McDowell, Ronald Schleifer, and Alan Velie, under the title *Structural Semantics: An Attempt at a Method.* Lincoln: University of Nebraska Press.

———. 1970. *Du sens.* Paris: Editions du Seuil.

Grimaud, Michel. 1978. "Sur une métaphore métonymique hugolienne selon Jacques Lacan." *Littérature* 29.

Groeben, Norbert. 1977. *Rezeptionsforschung als empirische Literaturwissenschaft.* Kronberg: Ts.

Hamon, Philippe. 1983. *Le personnel du roman. Le système des personnages dans les Rougons-Macquart de Zola.* Genève: Droz.

———. 1984. *Texte et idéologie.* Paris: P.U.F.

Heath, Stephen. 1982. *The Sexual Fix.* London: Macmillan.

Hendricks, William O. 1973. "Methodology of Narrative Structural Analysis." *Semiotica* 7.

Hulst, W. G. van der. 1976. *De Bijbelse Geschiedenissen.* Leiden: Spruyt, van Mantgem en De Does.

Iser, Wolfgang. 1972. *Der Implizite Leser.* München: Fink. English translation: *The Implied Reader: Patterns of Communication from Bunyan to Beckett.* Baltimore: Johns Hopkins University Press.

Jameson, Fredric. 1981. *The Political Unconscious: Narrative as a Socially Symbolic Act.* Ithaca: Cornell University Press.

Jauss, Hans Robert. 1975. "Racines und Goethes Iphigenie—Mit einem Nachwort über die Rezeptionsästhetischen Methode." In *Rezeptionsästhetik: Theorie und Praxis,* ed. Rainer Warning. München: Fink.

Jefferson, Ann. 1983. "*Mise en abyme* and the Prophetic in Narrative." *Style* 17, 2: 196–208.

Keller, Evelyn Fox. 1983. *Reflections on Gender and Science.* New Haven: Yale University Press.

Klink, Dr. Y. L. 1973. *Bijbel voor de kinderen. Het Oude Testament.* Amsterdam: Wereldvenster.

Knights, L. C. 1964. "How Many Children Had Lady MacBeth?" In *Explorations.* New York: New York University Press.

Kramer, S. N., ed. 1961. *Mythologies of the Ancient World.* New York: Anchor Books.

Kugel, James. 1981. *The Idea of Biblical Poetry.* New Haven: Yale University Press.

Kuyt, Evert. 1977. *Kinderbijbel. Het Oude Testament.* Den Haag: Boekcentrum.

Labov, William. 1972. *Explorations in Semantic Theory.* The Hague: Mouton.

Lacan, Jacques. 1966. *Ecrits.* Paris: Editions du Seuil.

Leach, Edmund, and D. Alan Aycock. 1983. *The Structuralist Interpretation of Biblical Myth.* Cambridge: Cambridge University Press.

Lévi-Strauss, Claude. 1949. *Les structures élémentaires de la parenté.* Paris: Plon.

———. 1966. *Mythologiques.* Paris: Plon.

Lévinas, Emmanuel. 1973. "Leçon talmudique." Congrès juif mondial, *L'autre dans la conscience juive.* Paris: P.U.F.

Lotman, Jurij. 1977. *The Structure of the Artistic Text.* Translated by Ronald Vroon. Ann Arbor: Michigan Slavic Publications.

Mailloux, Stephen. 1978. "The Red Badge of Courage and Interpretive Conventions: Critical Response to a Maimed Text." *Studies in the Novel* 10.

Malinowski, B. 1948. *Magic, Science and Religion and Other Essays.* New York: W. W. Norton.

Minski, Marvin. 1975. "A Framework for Representing Knowledge." In *The Psychology of Computer Vision,* edited by Patrick H. Winston. New York: McGraw-Hill.

Mooij, A. W. 1975. *Taal en verlangen. Lacans theorie van de psychoanalyse.* Meppel: Boom.

Naastepad, Th. I. M. 1975. *Simson.* Kampen: Kok.

O'Flaherty, Wendy Donger. 1980. *Women, Androgynes, and Other Mythical Beasts.* Chicago: University of Chicago Press.

Oosten, Jarich, and David Moyer. 1982. "De mythische omkering: een analyse van de sociale code van de scheppingsmythen van Genesis 2–11." *Anthropologische verkenningen* I, 1.

Peirce, Charles Sanders. 1931–35. *Collected Papers.* Edited by Charles Hartshorn and Paul Weiss. Cambridge: Harvard University Press.

Perry, Menakhem. 1979. "How the Order of a Text Creates its Meaning." *Poetics Today* 1–2.

Perry, Menakhem, and Meir Sternberg. 1968. "The King Through Ironic Eyes." *Ha-Sifrut.* Published as "Gaps, Ambiguity and the Reading Process," in Meir Sternberg 1985 (page reference to this edition).

Phillips, John A. 1984. *Eve. The History of an Idea.* New York: Harper and Row.

Prince, Gerald. 1982. *Narratology: The Form and Functioning of Narrative.* Berlin, New York: Mouton.

Rank, Otto. 1924. *Le traumatisme de la naissance.* Paris: Payot (n.d.).

Reed, Evelyn. 1975. *Woman's Evolution: From Matriarchal Clan to Patriarchal Family*. New York: Pathfinders Press.

Ricardou, Jean. 1971. *Pour une théorie du nouveau roman*. Paris: Editions du Seuil.

Ricoeur, Paul. 1983. *Temps et récit*. Paris: Editions du Seuil. Translated under the title *Time and Narrative*. Toronto: University of Toronto Press, 1984.

Rimmon, Shlomith. 1977. *The Concept of Ambiguity: The Example of James*. Chicago: University of Chicago Press.

Rimmon-Kenan, Shlomith. 1980. "The Paradoxical Status of Repetition." *Poetics Today* 1, 4.

———. 1983. *Narrative Fiction: Contemporary Poetics*. London: Methuen.

Sarraute, Nathalie. 1965. *L'ère du soupçon*. Paris: Gallimard.

Scholes, Robert, and Robert Kellog. 1966. *The Nature of Narrative*. Oxford: Oxford University Press.

Schor, Naomi. 1984. *Breaking the Chain: Feminism, Theory and French Realist Fiction*. New York: Columbia University Press.

Speiser, E. A. 1964. *Genesis*. The Anchor Bible. Garden City, New York: Doubleday.

Sternberg, Meir. 1985. *The Poetics of Biblical Narrative: Ideological Literature and the Drama of Reading*. Bloomington: Indiana University Press.

Tamir, Nomi. 1976. "Personal Narrative and its Linguistic Foundation." *PTL* 1, 3.

Trible, Phyllis. 1978. *God and the Rhetoric of Sexuality*. Philadelphia: Fortress Press.

Turner, Victor. 1969. *The Ritual Process: Structure and Anti-Structure*. Ithaca: Cornell University Press.

Uebersfeld, Anne. 1974. *Le roi et le bouffon*. Paris: José Corti.

Vries, Anne de. 1973. *Groot vertelboek voor de Bijbelse Geschiedenis*. Kampen: Kok.

Warner, Marina. 1976. *Alone of All Her Sex: The Myth and Cult of the Virgin Mary*. New York: Vintage Books.

Weber, Samuel. 1982. *The Legend of Freud*. Minneapolis: University of Minnesota Press.

Weinsheimer, Joel. 1979. "Theory of Character: Emma." *Poetics Today* 1, 1–2.

Westermann, C. 1966. *Genesis 1–11*. Neukirchen-Vluyn: Neukirchner Verlag.

Wolff, Hans Walter. 1974. *Anthropology of the Old Testament*. Philadelphia: Fortress Press.

INDEX

MIEKE BAL is Susan B. Anthony Professor of Women's Studies and Professor of Comparative Literature at the University of Rochester.